ANDERSON'S RULES

Books by Bob Anderson
Sarge, What Now?
Grandfather Speaks

TAC Leader Series
#1: What Honor Requires
#2: Night Hawks
#3: Retribution

**Books by
Jerry Ahern, Sharon Ahern and Bob Anderson**

The Survivalist Series
#30: The Inheritors of Earth
#31: Earth Shine
#32: The Quisling Covenant
The Shades of Love (Short Story)
Once Upon a Time (Short Story)
Light Dreams (Short Story)

Rourke Chronicles Series
#1: Everyman

**For more exciting
Books, eBooks, Audiobooks and more visit us at**
www.speakingvolumes.us

ANDERSON'S RULES

Bob Anderson

SPEAKING VOLUMES, LLC
NAPLES, FLORIDA
2014

Anderson's Rules

Editing assistance provided by Pamela Anderson.

ISBN 978-1-62815-215-9

DEDICATION

This book is dedicated to John and Shelley, my children—I love you and I am very proud of you; and to my grandchildren—Sarah, Rachel, Kayleigh, Josh and Seth—remember to love large and laugh often. I hope you see challenges not obstacles. Remember to believe in you—especially when no one else does.

It is also dedicated to Joel David who taught me karate, and to my students who taught me even more. To Richard Bach who taught me the power of blue feathers. To George King who reminded me that magic is a necessary part of every endeavor.

Lastly, this book is dedicated to my wife, Pam, whose place in my life is non-negotiable.

ACKNOWLEDGMENTS

As a baby boomer and a child of the sixties, my generation was promised more and received more than any other generation. Some folks say we also accomplished more, not all of it good. It has also been said that we did more drugs and that we tried to kill God.

We certainly challenged every concept handed down to us. Many of us were eager to believe in magic and science but nothing else. Many accepted Eric Von Daniken's book *Chariot of the Gods,* but rejected the Bible.

Some thought free sex meant we would find more love; we didn't. We thought that absolute freedom was the ultimate goal; instead, it became the atomic bomb of the human spirit.

There is a thin line between magic and delusion, and my bewildered generation crossed it many times.

One day I realized that I had crossed over and had to find my way back; but in order to find my way back, I first had to figure out where I was. I also needed an idea of where I wanted to go. Lastly, I felt it was imperative to determine whether or not I believed in anything anymore; and if so, what.

The only thing I was sure of was that I did not like where I was. Thus began a period of discovering and relearning. I found through books by Richard Bach both the guidance and direction that helped me believe that I could be successful in my quest.

I found through the martial arts a way to expend physical energy and gain spiritual strength, but I also found that much of the way I lived my life did not work. I discovered also that God was not dead, he was just being ignored.

I eventually found my way back and the successes I have enjoyed bear witness to the blessings that have been bestowed on me.

Early on as a public speaker, I've had many people ask me, "Do you have your philosophy written down?" I didn't. For years I had been quoting "Anderson's Rules," but had never bothered to put them down on paper.

I found that once I had them down on paper, it was easier to focus on how to describe them. As the essays developed, it became obvious that this process was not as static as simply making a compilation of rules.

People and life are not that static. People are fluid and change daily, sometimes hourly. Yet the more they change, the more they remain the same. Life is really pretty simple; we're supposed to live it. It becomes complicated and difficult when we don't make good solid decisions.

Many times we try to bend the universe to our own will. Many times we look for shortcuts to success and happiness—RARELY does it work.

Many times we don't have enough experience to see the pitfalls of our own actions. Someone once said that good judgment comes from bad experiences—they were right.

I want to acknowledge some of the folks that have helped me develop my philosophy. Some were friends; some were not but each of them came into my life to teach me something. Unfortunately, often it was something I did not want to learn.

I give credit to my parents, Buddy and Jinnie Ve Anderson. It's interesting how they became a lot smarter as I got older. I give credit to their generation, to the aunts and uncles that let me visit in their world; a world that enabled me to create my own world when I was old enough.

Thanks to my family, friends and those that I have loved, but especially to those individuals I have called "enemy." They probably have more to do with my successes than anyone else.

PREFACE

I have always believed that true wisdom is simple. After years of trying to understand the Eastern philosophy of Zen, I came across a sentence that said "What is—is." In that moment, I understood more about Zen than I had derived from all of the volumes and essays I had read in the past.

Being me, I expanded the thought to "What is—is, ergo what ain't—ain't." Years later I modified it again to "It is what it is till it ain't that no more!"

See, reality is the salient point. It did not matter how I wished things to be. What was important was how things really were. If I didn't like things the way they were, I had two choices: I could accept the way things were or I could change them if I had enough courage, ability and most important of all—enough "want power." The secret to this was embracing the conditions or situation. By embracing the challenges, I found my options became open and obvious.

Had I simply accepted the conditions or situation, I became a victim of it. By embracing the reality and then finding options, I became a victor over it.

I believe true wisdom must have a bit of the ironic and the humorous in it. Today's world is filled with so much drama that to say it can be intimidating is an understatement.

I define drama as needless chaos. I call folks that incorporate needless chaos in their lives and create it in the lives of others "soap opera people." I'll talk more about this in the book.

As hard as I have tried, I can't imagine a God that would create difficulty and horrific circumstances so his children could fail. I can imagine a God that would allow his children to become stronger by overcoming adversity. The problem is that most of us don't appreciate the challenge of challenges until we are older.

A while back I was in our nation's capital teaching a course for the military. As I drove along the Beltway in Washington D.C., an interesting thought bubbled up to my consciousness: I had become exactly who I always wanted to be.

That is not to say I have not made mistakes—I have. That is not to say that everything in my life has been rosy—it has not. That is not to say I am "full of myself"—I am not.

I believe that it is the failures I have experienced, the mistakes that I have made, the disasters I have endured, that have helped forge me into the person I am. People ask me, "What would you change in your life?" My answer is simple—nothing. Now, if I could go back in time, there are some things I would probably do more of, but that would be the only change.

I have had to learn from the mistakes I made. Had I not made them, had I not been embarrassed by them, I would not have learned.

Everything that has happened in my life has conspired to make me the person I am today. And today, I like me. There are many things I am proud of in my life. I have a wonderful wife, two wonderful children and five wonderful grandchildren.

I've had wonderful careers. I have dear and treasured friends, and I also have valued enemies. Each obstacle, each failure has challenged me. Each has tested me. Each has presented obstacles that forced me out of my comfort zone and into a reality that is better than any fantasy could be.

Over the years, I have tried to follow and to teach the rules I will share in this book. Like a song says, "it may not work for you, but it works for me." I hope that something in this book will connect with a need you have.

There is nothing new in this book because "All thoughts that can be thought have been thought—I think." Having said that, I believe that it is essential that each of us continue to explore what are "new" thoughts for us.

Maybe my "twist" will touch something in you that will allow you to see the wonder of your own life in a different light. Maybe the irony or the humor of my presentation will slant your perception of the challenges in your own life.

If so, you may be able to recognize those circumstances not as obstacles, but as opportunities to grow. Growth is inevitable, but it is also relative. Not everyone grows at the same rate. Not everyone excels in the same things. Not everyone succeeds in the same way.

My generation was told, "You're special." I don't believe that anymore. I do believe, however, that we are each unique. Our uniqueness is forged by our circumstances, our abilities, but mostly by our attitudes.

I've known folks who when faced with significant challenges such as serious disease, serious injury, death of loved ones and all manners of illness, became victims of those calamities.

I've known others who have faced the same obstacles and became victors over adversity—same circumstances but different outcomes—simply because of their attitudes.

I remember hearing Earl Nightingale talk about twin brothers. Their father was a violent and mean drunk. When the twins grew up they went their separate ways.

One went to the east coast and became a highly successful business man. The other brother went to the west coast and became a bum.

Years later, the successful brother was scheduled to receive a prestigious award. A columnist tracked down the other brother for an interview. The same question was asked to both brothers, "Why has your life turned out the way it did?" Curiously, both brothers gave the same answer, "With a father like mine, what choice did I have?"

FOREWORD

Bob is a warrior. In an earlier time and place, he might have been a Samurai. He is my Sensei (Teacher) in Shorin Ryu Karate—we played together in his "sandbox" for over fifteen years. Since you are reading this book, you may be interested in some things I have learned from Sensei Bob about the martial arts and life.

The Universe is Our Sacred Dojo

In our case, the "sandbox" is our Dojo (training hall) and Bob stressed that the Dojo can be any place we come together. It is a sacred place and we express our respect by a silent bow to the place and to each other when we enter or depart.

We Are Responsible for our Actions

Kumite (light contact contest) with other students was our reward when we performed well with basic moves in the Kata. Bob insisted we respect each other with a bow to begin and end the Kumite. Control in all techniques was required. We learned to be responsible for control of our techniques. Violations meant we had to Kumite with Sensei Bob, so violations were very rare.

Whatever We Do—Do It With Passion

KATAS (pre-arranged movements) taught us techniques which we did not recognize as such until much later in our training. Bob would not tolerate students being "half-hearted" in performing the KATA movements. "Show me that you see the attacker coming upon you, move with intensity as if your life depended upon it." He would quote the great Samurai Kendo Master

Musashi: "move in like your hair is on fire." We learned to do the KATA moves with passion.

Focus On The Present Moment

When we came together in the Dojo, we always sat for a few minutes in a meditative position. Bob always reminded us: "empty your mind; leave outside the door all worldly cares. Come to this place at this time with an empty cup that may be filled with whatever is useful. Focus all your Ki (Life Force) only on the present moment—which is the point in the martial arts world at which life or death hangs in the balance."

I have come to know that the Universe is Sensei Bob's "Dojo/Sandbox." It is a place to learn and to play. Consider how many life experiences fit into those two categories. In reading this book, you are invited into Sensei Bob's Dojo. Please enter with an "empty cup" and leave the door open for others. Have a great adventure—Kumite!

George King
—Shodan
—Shorin-Ryu

TABLE OF CONTENTS

RULE 1

When faced with difficult decisions remember this: It is not important what you decide—it is only important what you decide about what you decided.

Decision making is often difficult. Oh, it is not that bad when the options are vastly different. Do I accept a job that is everything I want, the money is good, the hours are short and I don't have to learn anything new? Or do I stay where I am, unhappy, underpaid, working long hours with no appreciation? A simple choice, right?

In psychology I learned about three conditions. They are as follows:

1. approach/approach
2. avoidance/avoidance
3. approach/avoidance

Approach/approach—this can mean that both alternatives are attractive to you or that you can deal realistically with your options head on. I have two choices, either of which is acceptable. This can also be called win/win.

Avoidance/avoidance—this can mean that both alternatives are unattractive or that you're not dealing with reality. You are hoping things will simply change even if nothing is done to change it. You have two choices, neither of which is acceptable. This can also be called lose/lose.

The greatest difficulties are in the approach/avoidance scenario—both decisions have elements of winning and losing. In

1

simpler terms, we sit down and start listing out the pros and cons—the good things about both decisions and the bad things about both decisions.

In the end, the two lists are almost identical. Or one is ahead of the other in tangible elements, such as money or fringe benefits. But the other is ahead in intangibles, such as perceived honor, less stress, etc. These types of decisions form what have been called "The Horns of a Dilemma."

Both decisions could be good. Both decisions could be bad. This is where my first rule applies. When faced with difficult decisions remember this: It is not important what you decide—it is only important what you decide about what you decided.

It becomes a matter of your attitude about the circumstances you have or will create. If you decide it is the worst job in the world, it will be. If you decide you can't be happy with the choice, you won't be. If you decide the tasks are too difficult and you will fail, you will. Furthermore, you will find a legion of individuals that will be happy to enhance your failure.

Remember the adage, "Misery loves company?" Most folks do not like to see you happy, simply because they are not happy. Most folks do not like to see you succeed, because they don't feel that they have succeeded.

If you fail, they are freed of the aspects of having to improve their circumstances. Now understand, this is not based in viciousness; it is based in laziness. See, if you succeed, it could force them to examine their own lives to determine why they have not been successful. Most folks don't want to do that.

They favor a path of reduced expectations—they will just denigrate you for your successes. It's easier than changing their circumstances.

Several years ago, I was promoted to the position of training director for a major plant. It was a job that I worked for and wanted very badly, and was fortunate enough to get.

During the first two months people would ask, "How's it going?" My standard answer was, "If it was any better, I couldn't stand it!"

After a couple of months, I noticed people looked at me funny. I was having the time of my life in my job and loved going to work every day. I started to realize I was making people uncomfortable with my enthusiasm.

I started answering the question with a more acceptable response, "It's okay." Within just weeks, this wonderful job became—okay. I was no longer happy to go to work; it had become just another job. However, I was accepted more easily by those co-workers that could not understand how happy I had been.

One day I realized that I had allowed these folks to steal my joy. That was wrong, but it was my own fault. I did not understand the dynamics of protecting my own joy versus fitting in with others.

I do not believe that feelings determine your behavior. I believe the reverse to be true—your behavior determines your feelings. Years ago, Dale Carnegie said, "Act enthusiastic and you will be enthusiastic." He was right.

Anderson's first rule is based on the simple premise that two people can be faced with exactly the same decision and circumstances and the same abilities and qualifications. One will choose option (A) and be miserable. The other will choose option (A) and be extremely successful and happy. The difference—Attitude!

Remember this: When faced with options that are not clear cut, when the pros and cons are nearly balanced, when faced with difficult decisions, it is not important what you decide, it is only important what you decide about what you decided.

Bob Anderson

Anderson's Thought

All dilemmas have aspects of good and bad, beauty and ugliness, grace and turmoil.

What determines the good, the beauty or the grace, is your own attitude and willingness to "own" your decision and make the best of it.

RULE 2

You are never ready for anything until you have been in it for a while.

While writing this book, I sent this essay to George King to read and give me feedback. When George was writing the Foreword, he told me that "the magic" wasn't coming through in my first attempt. He asked if I was saying not to try. That definitely was not what I was trying to convey.

Several years ago, I was teaching a Karate class and was fortunate to have George come in as a student. He was 57 at the time and the oldest student I had ever had.

George was in great shape. He was a runner and routinely ran half marathons, and occasionally a full one. It was George who introduced me to Richard Bach and the book, *Illusions—The Adventures of a Reluctant Messiah.*

George is, without exception, the most "spiritual" man I had ever met. Throughout our entire relationship, he has maintained a "center" that few people ever experience, even for a short time.

When George first started in my class, he had that typical "stiffness" that many runners develop. He was unable to complete a proper kick higher than six inches off the ground. If he tried to go higher, he would lose his technique.

Three years later, I was sparring with him and conversing with another student at the same time. "Old George" had great hand technique and I knew to watch them, but his feet were never a threat, until that day.

While I was talking, out of the corner of my eye I saw George set up for a round house kick; and without much thought, I blocked his kick at about waist level. However, his foot impacted the right side of my chest, not my waist.

He had kicked at least eight inches higher than he ever had before, with perfect technique. I was seeing stars as I realized I probably had a couple of cracked ribs. He rushed to see if I was okay and felt tremendous sorrow that he had hurt me.

My comment, albeit through clenched teeth and broken breath was, "Good kick, George."

If I have been his Sensei, he has been my Guru, my Messiah. He is a "magician" of the highest order. Simply put, this means he has both the ability to make magical things happen and to see when magic is missing. He is the closest thing I have ever met to Don Shimodo from the book *Illusions*.

George and I talked about the lack of magic in this essay and, as so often happens when I speak with George, I could see what I was not looking at or looking for. He reminded me that this life is a sandbox and that the world is our Dojo.

I find that many people are turned off or fearful of the martial arts. They say it's "too physical and teaches you how to fight." Actually, martial arts should teach you when to fight.

It is easy to learn how to punch and how to kick. What is more important is to learn when you should punch or kick, and when you should avoid the opportunity. There are times when it is necessary to fight. These include defending yourself or someone else or defending what you believe in.

There are also times when the correct thing to do is not to fight. Instead of employing a roundhouse kick, it may be more appropriate to negotiate. Sometimes it is necessary to turn your back on challenges that involve physical threats, as long as you know the difference between walking away and running away.

I have found that many people seek challenges from the bleachers and the stands. They watch someone else doing something that they think they want to do. The problem is that they are watching someone do something they have been doing for a while.

That person has practiced and refined their process. That process may be martial arts, management, sports, marriage or just living. It is impossible to see how much time and effort was expended in developing the skills and technique to "make it look easy."

It is impossible to know how many times they failed, how many times they screwed it up. It is impossible to see the effort it took to make the magic. Therefore, when the watcher gets off the bleachers and begins to do this thing, it is common that the person will falter or screw it up.

It's a lot harder to do something than it is to watch something. All or most of the mistakes the doer made, the watcher will probably make as he or she begins to become the doer.

It is only when you move out of the bleachers, off the side line, into the pit where a particular task is performed, and you start performing that task, that you understand the intricacies of the task, whatever that task may be.

So often we hear folks say, "I'm ready for that job" or "I am ready to become" or "I am ready to accept ..." Ladies and gentlemen, recognize you probably are not ready. The reason: you have been sitting in the bleachers, on the side lines, in another job or circumstance, and all you have seen is that which is visible.

How often have you seen someone pursue a goal of a new job, attain that goal only to fail at the job? The reason is they did not know what else was associated with that job. They COULD not see the things they did not see.

7

These "things" may be intangible, things that the person currently in that job can't display. This is not to say they were deceived, but maybe the incumbent spent a long time perfecting his or her abilities in that job. He or she will make it look easy because they know how to do it.

To do anything well, you must perform that thing correctly. Simply watching someone perform that operation does not give you a feel for what it is like to actually perform that operation. It is only when you are the one "doing the deed" that you learn whatever it was that you did not see.

For example, I am in awe of anyone with musical talent. It amazes me to watch someone play any instrument and particularly those that can play several instruments. They make it look so easy. They make it look fun. They make it look effortless. I, on the other hand, have trouble playing the radio.

Several years ago, I decided I would play the guitar. I struggled, my fingers hurt, by back hurt, my ears hurt. The ears of everyone around me also hurt. It was not effortless, it was work. Eventually I stopped. I did not realize how much work it would be.

Further, it is only after you have been performing the task for a period of time that you can appreciate ALL of the issues involved in it. Therefore, for simplicity's sake, I say: You are never ready for anything until you have been in it for a while. The time is different for each person and each task, but six weeks is a good starting point.

This includes a new job, a new career, a new class, a new hobby, a new friendship, or evaluating someone that you would consider a potential mate.

Don't judge the success of it for at least six weeks. It's like a probationary period—you are trying it out to see how it works. It takes a while to get your bearings, to know what you have gotten yourself into. What is required for you to be successful. You can't be successful at something until you first know what you are dealing with.

Don't give up that first week because it's hard. Stick with it, because with time, commitment, and practice the task will become easier, or you'll find out it's not right for you. For commitment's sake, I say "give it your all for six weeks."

In six weeks you'll be a better judge to determine that IT (whatever IT is) has potential and is worth the investment of your time, or that it doesn't.

You may reevaluate in another six months, then again in another six months. This is how we measure success. Over time, it is necessary to determine if we are improving our situation or if we are sitting stagnant.

If you are not sure you'll like something, give it six weeks. It takes at least six weeks of dating to start to really get to know someone. At the end of those six weeks, you can determine if you like that person or not. It's the "stick-to-it-ive-ness" that will lead to success.

It's those six weeks, six months or six years that a person stumbles through, without all of the knowledge, ability and capacity that will ultimately make that person successful; if they want it bad enough. If they don't, they will QUIT!

George wanted to become good at martial arts. For a long time he could not bend well, could not kick well, and his movements were stiff and mechanical. He failed at many of the tasks he attempted. He could not do many of the things that I required him to do. He had reasons for his failures, his age being one of them. He was inexperienced. He did not seek combat or competition.

The bumblebee has been scientifically proven to be physically unable to fly, but no one ever told the bumblebee. George had

9

reasons for failing in karate but, like the bumblebee, no one ever told George he could not fly. He wanted to be successful and he was willing to do those things that were necessary—so he became successful.

George did not compete with the younger students. He had to make that journey on his own and he did. He obtained his black belt almost ten years after he started the pursuit of that goal.

While he had support from the class, it was up to him to accomplish what he found out was a lot harder than he originally thought. And that is the way it is for all of us.

Anderson's Thought

Every human endeavor involves more than it appears to. The easier it appears to be, the more there is that is hidden.

Triumph does not come from the first attempt. Triumph comes AFTER overcoming the difficult and complex.

Triumph arrives when, "What can be, becomes real."

RULE 3

Practice does not make perfect. Practice makes permanent— but improvement will come through doing it right, repeatedly.

One of my favorite and most requested presentations is called "Excellence Ain't Easy." It is a silly title to a very serious subject. Too often in today's world, we accept mediocrity when excellence is just around the corner.

There is an old adage, "Practice makes perfect." It is incorrect. Practice makes permanent. If you practice anything incorrectly long enough, you will perfectly perform the task— incorrectly.

If you do not understand all of the aspects of what you are doing, I will guarantee that you will miss some critical step in the process that you did not see.

As a student of the martial arts, I had to learn katas. Katas are choreographed sets of movements that involve all aspects of the body—the hands, arms, body, legs, feet and head. They look like dances, yet they are not dances. They are highly developed processes that exercise the mind and body in a variety of circumstances. They prepare you for combat by teaching you what moves to make under each circumstance.

There is a flow to a kata; there is a purpose to the kata. However, to the inexperienced or uninitiated person, it is impossible to understand what the purpose of each movement is when viewed as part of the whole system. One particular hand movement looks like a wave but isn't—it simulates a grabbing technique.

11

When a person is grabbed, that person will resist and the grabber must be prepared to meet that resistance. Therefore, balance at the start of the movement is important or you can be pulled off balance by the opponent.

Once you understand the purpose of the movement and how it relates to other movements, you have the knowledge to develop your skills properly. Once you understand the proper technique, the proper application, the proper countermove, you add significantly to your success quotient.

Practice does not make perfect. However, it could be said that perfect practice makes perfect.

Perfect practice happens when practice is observed by someone with more knowledge and skill than you, who can identify improper technique or mistakes. When these mistakes are corrected and repeated, improvement occurs.

The more often you do it correctly, the faster you will become, the stronger you will become, the better at it you will be—you will obtain excellence.

It is a natural process that occurs when the correct techniques and processes are repeated and are combined with a commitment to stick to it.

As mentioned before, we need time to be actively involved with something in order to truly understand what we are involved with. We need correction and sometimes we perceive correction as criticism.

As my wife Pam says, "We can't be successful without others. We have to have others critique us—this is life! That's why kids who get everything they want and don't have to earn any of it, are going to be faced with a hard reality when they are expected to act as responsible and productive adults. Their parents have done them no favors. Therefore, we have to humble ourselves and prepare ourselves for criticism and critique, and only we can decide what we do with it. We will either become bitter or better."

Anderson's Thought

Learning and improvement takes place during the development of skills and abilities. This is called the "doing" and it is difficult.

The "done" is when we have accomplished the task we set for our self.

"Done" is to be celebrated.

RULE 4

You can't change anybody except yourself. Change you and you change everything.

One of the greatest mistakes we as humans make is trying to change other people. This is like trying to teach a bull to sing. It does not work and it makes the bull mad.

I have heard it said that a man finds a woman to marry and hopes she never changes. A woman finds a man to marry hoping to change him. Ain't that a mess?

Years ago I thought, "I can change the world. It is so obvious what the problems are." When I first began studying psychology I was thrilled. I thought, "I have found the secrets. Now I can fix these folks that are so messed up." Wrong.

First of all, to "fix" someone meant to correct their behavior or life. The question became: Correct to what standard—mine or theirs? If I tried to correct their lives to my standard, who had died and made me king?

If I tried to correct their lives to their own standard, that did not work either. Most were exactly where they wanted to be. Or, more accurately, they were where they had chosen to be because they did not want to do what was necessary to change where they were. I found out in short order I could not "fix" them.

It was not that I did not want to help them. It was not that I could not define the problems and offer guidance on how to change their lives and fix their world.

Their problem was that they were not willing to do what was necessary to change their lives. I also found that very few people would admit to this.

14

The turmoil in their lives had become "normal." Their lives had always been screwed up. They continued to make bad choices because those were the only choices they thought they had.

Invariably, the "fixes" were simple steps, but those steps would require them to get way out of their comfort zones. It might mean they would have to dissolve relationships that were poisonous to them.

It might mean that they would have to take steps that would create a new reality. It might mean that they would have to "work" to fix their own problems. There were many explanations as to why my suggestions would not work.

Most people find it easier to pop a pill than to deal with a problem. In fact, this is encouraged through ads and commercials, and seen as a sign of success and acceptance by most people today.

As my wife says, "Many people base their happiness on others. They say 'if only my husband would do this or that, I would be happy. If only my boss did this or that, then I would be happy.' The reality is when you are looking externally for happiness, you'll never attain it. The 'if only' mindset will absolutely doom you and those around you to misery."

I have found that, first of all, you have to "see" success. Only when you have a clear view of what "good" looks like can you emulate it. Some people have the ability to see things that have not yet happened. There is a saying, "only those that can see the invisible can accomplish the impossible."

Roger Banister, Edmund Hillary and Tenzing Norgay are three such people. It was considered a medically accepted "fact" that if a man ran a mile in less than four minutes, his heart would explode. This "fact" was destroyed in May of 1954 when Roger Banister broke the four minute mile.

Hillary and Norgay knew no man had ever climbed Mount Everest and lived to tell about it—until they did it in February of 1953.

Today, the four minute mile is often broken and you can book tours to climb Mount Everest. All because these three men could see the invisible; therefore, they accomplished the impossible.

The second element of success is that you have to believe that you can accomplish the goal. This involves training and self-improvement. No one can simply face an obstacle and overcome it on the first try.

Remember rule two? "You are never ready for anything until you have been in it for at least six weeks." Understand that "six weeks" is simply a reference point, a concept. Depending on the individual and the task, it could be six minutes, six hours, six days or six months. The point is that it takes time to understand the nuances of what you are doing.

It may involve academic education to acquire the knowledge necessary. It may involve physical conditioning to get to the point that you are ready for the strenuous activity.

No one wakes up one morning, decides they are going to become a Navy SEAL or a Green Beret, goes out that evening and passes the course. It takes dedication to do what is necessary to pass that course.

No one wakes up one morning, decides that they want to become a medical doctor, goes out that evening and obtains a medical degree. It takes years of struggle and sacrifice, and not everyone is up for that degree of challenge.

Here is a fact for you—THE WORLD IS NOT FAIR! The world does not care what you want in your life. The world only cares whether or not you want it bad enough, to do the things necessary to accomplish the goal.

If you do what is necessary to the level required, you can be the winner! People talk a lot about will power. I personally think will power is garbage. The only power that has any association with success is WANT power.

Do I want it—whatever it is—badly enough to do all of the things necessary to accomplish it? If I do, then I will—as long as I don't quit.

The final step for attaining success is answering the question, "Am I worthy of success?" Most folks do not consider themselves worthy of success, therefore they fail. These people will employ WILL power in the pursuit of success. They almost always fail.

Only those folks that SEE success, WANT success bad enough to do what is necessary, and FEEL worthy of the success, WIN!

The world and all of the people around you—and most importantly you—will find all manner of reasons not to try harder or not to be successful.

It is easy to quit. It is difficult to succeed and more difficult to excel. If it were easy, anybody could do it.

My wife, who has a Master's degree in Education says, "In fact, we are teaching our kids not to excel. We want to protect kids from disappointment and failure. Many schools have taken 'Excellent' off of report cards because it might hurt the feelings of other students that did not get an E for excellence. How sad this is. Let's justify and sanctify mediocrity rather than hold excellence out as a goal. The world has taken the satisfactory mindset; just do enough to be considered satisfactory. It won't get you fired, but sure won't get you any higher."

I sincerely believe that most folks will attain the level of success that they are willing to attain. Remember, success means different things to different people.

Happiness means different things to different people and having the right "tools" alone just doesn't "do it." Tools will not make you successful. Only you can do that.

I know people with a formal education that are idiots—they have no common sense. I know people who have attained success and could not maintain it. I know bums that have been to the top of the corporate ladder and flopped.

I have also seen folks use drugs, sex and gambling to destroy what they spent a lifetime creating. The reason again is simple: They did not consider themselves worthy of that success.

They had been successful, sometimes in spite of their worst efforts. Sometimes, when they became successful, they no longer felt they could sustain that success.

In any event, when a person does not or no longer considers himself to be worthy of the successes he has earned, that person will destroy those successes. In the process, he will generally hurt or destroy those people that helped him become successful in the first place.

Anderson's Thought

There is positive and negative energy in the world.

Trying to change another person to think, behave or be what we want of them creates negative energy, and it doesn't work.

I can positively change myself. That is positive energy, and that's the real source of happiness.

RULE 5

The job of a leader is to remember Anderson's Rule of Large Numbers.

I don't know very many people that get up in the morning with the attitude of, "Hey, let's see how bad I can screw up my life today." I don't know very many people that wake up and decide, "I've got a great idea, let's see if I can get fired today." I don't know very many people that get up and decide, "You know, I think I'll see if I can destroy my family today," but believe it or not, there are some.

Most folks shy away from unneeded turmoil in their life. Most folks want to do "good" and most will do "good," if they know what "good" looks like. Some folks need a little more help to become functionally adept at their job, their career, and their familial responsibilities. They are not trying to mess up; they probably just don't have a clear view of what "good" looks like.

I see this often in business and industry as well as in the military. The boss gets frustrated and decides to fire an employee that is not measuring up. I don't have a problem with that. What I have a problem with is when the boss never developed the employee, never showed that person what they expected. I have a problem when a boss does not give feedback to an employee so they can correct mistakes or shortcomings.

For years I have dealt with employees who have no job descriptions, employees that have never had a performance evaluation or employees that believe they are doing their job well—until the day they are fired.

19

Supervisors and managers need to "parent" their subordinates. It is like dealing with your children. The child who is told "clean up your room" may pick up five toys and feel they have done exactly what the parent wanted.

If the parent means "pick up every toy and vacuum the room," that parent needs to convey that message in terms the child can understand. The same is true of supervisors and managers; the same is also true of spouses.

My wife, Pam, will ask me to take out the trash. I respond, "Certainly, Dear." My response means to me that I'll take out the trash as soon as this show is over and if you'll kindly remind me at least once more.

To Pam, her instruction meant, "Now please!"

I was not trying to fail, I just did not understand what she was asking. She was not trying to be difficult, she did not understand what I meant by "Certainly, Dear." It is simply a matter of more effective communication.

If we want something from someone else, we must be clear in setting correct expectations, AND we must have agreement on those expectations from both parties. This holds true in most of our dealings.

I have used Anderson's Rule of Large Numbers for over twenty years, to teach managers and supervisors a particular point. Specifically, Anderson's Rule of Large Numbers says that eighty-five percent of your people will give you their very best the very first time. Ten percent will require more training and more guidance but they also will perform well.

That leaves five percent. Of that five, three percent of the people will try your patience and require extraordinary efforts in the areas of communications and boundary setting, but will be successful if enough effort is exerted by the parent, supervisor or spouse.

They are difficult to direct, but when they get it—THEY GOT IT. They will be your elite. They have enough courage to challenge the system. They will not just be successful—they will be highly successful. They will excel.

The remaining two percent will never function in accordance with standards, boundaries or expectations. You will need to just shoot them and be done with it. They, for some reason, have made the conscious decision NOT to be successful and they will not allow you to make them successful.

Their disobedience, their criminal behavior, their unethical behavior, their cheating behavior, are all patterns that will be enforced by their personality. They will walk across the street in the rain to screw up, when they could stay indoors and be successful.

Pam is fond of adding, "Beware, they like to take others with them. Remember, misery loves company."

The job of an effective leader is not to handle the first eighty-five percent, they will handle themselves. It is not to handle the next ten percent, they just need a little help and that is usually an easy task. Their job is to tell the difference between the last three and two percent. Only then can they focus on providing the guidance that the three percent need in order to be outstanding and excel; and stop wasting time on the incorrigible two percent that have chosen to fail.

Anderson's Thought

A Manager manages things. A Leader leads people.
A Manager does things right. A Leader does right things.

RULE 6

Life is a pattern of choices between winning and losing. Choose to win!

As we go through life, each of us will face challenges that we should not take on, obstacles that we should not try to overcome, battles that we should not fight and games that we should not play.

For example, while I would like to break the four minute mile, I am not willing to do the things necessary to train for the attempt. I've decided I will break the four minute mile in my car! I love to run, but not at that level. Running at that level would take the fun out of it for me.

I know I am not willing to be successful at this task and that I do not want to do what would be necessary to become successful at this task.

I know that I would love to see the top of Mt. Everest. I also know that I am not willing to learn mountain climbing or to deal with the exhausting and dangerous aspects of climbing to the top of Everest. I can't imagine the thrill of standing on top of the world. Nor can I imagine freezing my rear off in a place where it takes an hour to move through thirty feet of space, while struggling for every breath.

I know I could do both of the tasks I listed above, but I know I don't "want" to do either.

By arriving at that decision, I have been successful—I have won. I can now focus my energy on things that I want to do and only those for which I am willing to do the things necessary to be successful. I know I cannot do everything I might have an interest in, so I would rather do the things I have a passion for.

There is no challenge in tackling obstacles easily overcome, but there is folly in wasting time on things at which I do not choose to be successful.

I have decided who and what I am going to be and I will pursue that with every bit of my being. That is how I am successful. Success should not be measured as a single accomplishment, but as a series of accomplishments.

Remember, "Even a blind hog will occasionally find an acorn!"

I want to be successful in many things, not one single thing. I remember when I came across the audio book *Flags of our Fathers,* by James Bradley. Mr. Bradley is the son of John Bradley, one of the men pictured in Joseph Rosenthal's magnificent picture of the raising the American flag at Mount Suribachi, on the island of Iwo Jima during World War II.

As I listened to the audio book, the best part for me was listening to his description of his father as a dad and as a man; not someone who allowed his legacy to be defined by a 1/400 of a second shutter speed on a camera.

Many of us (me included) would be tempted to be the "hero" of that picture. John Bradley, however, chose to be a man, a father, a community member, a loving friend, a loving spouse and a grandfather. He chose to live a life of service, not fame. He determined that the real heroes of Iwo Jima were the ones that never came home. He won and I salute him for his winning.

Anderson's Thought

Real courage and real winning sometimes look like fear and losing.

23

RULE 7

"Damned if you do and damned if you don't" are never equal—do what's right.

For a moment I would like to visit "the horns of the dilemma." Many times we arrive at a place where the term "Damned if you do and damned if you don't" can apply. I have found that these dilemmas usually involve some aspect of ethical or professional behavior. Initially, it is easy to miss the true question of such dilemmas.

When speaking to managers and supervisors, I always tell them that "Managers do things right and leaders do right things." Many times in my career, I have faced situations where I was expected to do a certain thing because the popular opinion said that is what should be done.

Often I have found that popular opinion is only popular with those who do not wish to be held accountable or responsible for that opinion.

I have also learned that "society" is a tool to prevent chaos from reigning in all human activities. We turn loose some degree of control as individuals in order to live in our "tribe." The tribe is one of the most basic social organizations.

The "tribe" is a collection of individuals that have decided to coexist, share challenges, share commodities, share hardships and share the benefits of coexisting. But it is the strength of each individual that sets the course and health of that tribe, that company, that city, that town or that family. It is the individual, not the tribe, which is the salvation of the tribe.

The tribe does not exist without the individuals in it. The tribe is a creation of man and I believe that it is essential; but, man is the creation of God and should not be dominated by the creation of man.

God gave us the burden of free will. God gave us the blessing of free will. Our responsibility to God and to the members of the tribe is to use that free will. To stand as a guardian of what is right—not what is convenient or easy.

We still live in tribes as our ancestors did, but today our villages are linked to the rest of the world in ways our forefathers would have never dreamed of. Our tribes are no longer groups of tens or hundreds or even thousands. Our tribes today are cities of hundreds of thousands or millions of people.

Some are not from our tribe, but have decided to live in the same area. Most do not share the same religious beliefs. Many can't yet speak the language. Many are criminal in their behavior. Our tribes are much more complex than in the past.

Yet in times of trouble, we unite. Each member of these tribes has their own particular, and often peculiar, view of what is right and appropriate. There is also a "tribe consciousness" of what that tribe believes is right or wrong. This consensus of opinion is expressed through laws, rules and communication between the tribal members.

Buddha said, "Life is hard." Sometimes it is necessary to stand alone against evil. If each individual does that, evil cannot flourish. Remember as Edmund Burke said, "All that is necessary for evil to triumph is for good men to do nothing."

Societies have no concept of true right. An example: In 1939 a society created fundamental concepts and laws that violated the rule of God and enslaved whole populations and exterminated millions of innocent men, women and children.

That "tribe" said it was okay. Some individuals in that tribe said, "No it is not and I will fight it, even at the cost of my life and my fortunes." The tribe was Germany, and it created the most powerful war machine the world had ever seen.

Many individuals, however, resisted the tide of that society's opinion. Schindler, Anne Frank and many others that history does not know by name, are forever honored for what they did and did not do.

They did what was right, in spite of what the rule of law and the rule of man said. They sided with God against oppression, anger and death—and won.

Anderson's Thought

Courage is not the absence of fear. Courage is doing the right thing in spite of your fear.

RULE 8

We do not learn from success—we celebrate it. We learn best from failure and embarrassment.

One of the basic tenants of human adult learning is that we learn from making mistakes and avoid making those same mistakes again. When we fail, and fail miserably, it is in that failing we make decisions that determine our own futures. We didn't like failing, so we avoid failing again by getting better at what we failed at.

When I was a child we used to play baseball in my neighborhood. Some of these kids were really good at baseball and were always picked first for the teams. Many of us were picked later or not at all. We were not that good at baseball.

The rule was simple: If you wanted to play, you had to learn to play better. Again, if you are willing to do what is necessary to be successful, you will be successful.

Treasure your failures. By failing, you find out where and what you need to improve. If you get out there and practice pitching, catching, fielding, and throwing and show improvement, you'll get picked for the team. If you don't practice and improve, you don't get picked.

It is as simple as that and remains a basic premise of the real world. Even attempts such as affirmative action could not override this premise. Those being discriminated against should not be given opportunities to succeed in spite of their abilities. Rather they should fight against established patterns of behavior by the majority of society—and win.

Later on, when presented with a level playing field, many individuals rose to the occasion and developed those skills necessary to keep that position and succeeded even further. And they did it on their own merit.

Many didn't and gradually those folks that did not take advantage of the opportunity, failed. Unfortunately, we continue to try to make the world fair. We continue to try to eliminate failure.

On the surface that does not sound too bad. I have failed and I hated it. It was embarrassing. It did not feel good. In reality the world is not fair; and if you eliminate failure, you eliminate excellence.

The ONLY way to be truly successful is to get an opportunity. I have always said, "Just give me an opportunity to show you what I can do."

Many other folks said that and, unfortunately, they showed us what they can (or can't) do. Many failed to continue developing themselves and they bastardized the process. They turned America into an "entitlement society" that believes society owed them something.

I believe that each individual is owed the opportunity to succeed. I do not believe every individual will, or SHOULD, be successful. The world does not work that way. Success is earned, not given. It is not a right, it is a privilege.

Excellence is the correspondent of failure—you cannot have one without the other. The attempt to eliminate failure will only eliminate excellence and homogenize the gene pool. We would then gain the dubious distinction of being able to be just like everyone else.

I don't want to be like anyone else. While there are many characteristics in many people that I value and strive to make mine, I am a unique creation of the Almighty. His task for me is to excel at being me.

Anderson's Rules

I am supposed to strive against odds and to succeed, not in spite of those odds, but because of them. The words to the song *"The Impossible Dream,"* written by Joe Darion, says it nicely:

To dream ... the impossible dream ...
To fight ... the unbeatable foe ...
To bear ... with unbearable sorrow ...
To run ... where the brave dare not go ...
To right ... the unrightable wrong ...
To love ... pure and chaste from afar ...
To try ... when your arms are too weary ...
To reach ... the unreachable star ...

This is my quest, to follow that star ...
No matter how hopeless, no matter how far ...
To fight for the right, without question
or pause ...
To be willing to march into Hell, for
a Heavenly cause ...
And I know if I'll only be true, to this
glorious quest,
That my heart will lie will lie peaceful
and calm, when I'm laid to my rest ...

And the world will be better for this:
That one man, scorned and covered
with scars,
Still strove, with his last ounce of courage,
To reach ... the unreachable star ...

We learn nothing from our successes, we are not supposed to. We are supposed to celebrate them.

We only learn through failure. Children learn by their successes. As we get older we learn to avoid punishment, embarrassment and failure.

Fortunately, or unfortunately, it is the way of things.

Anderson's Thought

It is the failures and bad things that have happened in your life that have made you who you are.

These are the things that have strengthened you and given you character.

RULE 9

I can't please anyone if I have not pleased me.

Again, referring to the tribe, we must remember that the tribe is a tool that mankind created to maintain order and increase his own chances of survival. As someone said, "You can't please everybody all of the time." The same issue will please one group and make another group angry. Why is this? Simple, everyone has their own way of looking at things.

Everyone has their own agenda and perspective. As in the martial arts, for every punch there is a block. For every block, there is a counter measure. This is also true of life.

For every good deed, there is a negative impact for someone. For every bad deed, there is someone who prospers. Remember, you are trying to live within the tribe and the tribe assumes its own personality.

For example, let's examine riots. When enough members of the tribe get together, their behavior changes. The tribe begins to behave in a manner that its individual members never would.

Being in that tribe allows you to become "invisible" and sometimes allows you not to be accountable. Remember that the tribe is made up of individuals. If you have a bunch of individuals, they can become a mob. That mob will kill, steal, and destroy, although none of the individuals would ever act that way on their own.

As individuals, if we are happy with ourselves, that happiness becomes a buffer that prevents the mob from ever forming. We have a group of individuals that can work together for the mutual goal and benefit of its members.

31

That is what a tribe should be—a grouping of individuals working together but secure within themselves.

Another basic premise of mankind is: "I can't make any other individual happy. I can only make myself happy. But if I am happy, another happy person will be drawn to that happiness."

Anderson's Thought

Why work diligently at something that when it's going as well as it possibly can, does not meet your needs?

Why not spend that energy enjoying something that completes your soul and meets your needs?

Don't do what feels good—do what makes YOU feel good as a person.

RULE 10

Never violate the Rule of Ego.

Years ago, I created what I now call the Rule of Ego. It says simply, "Never, ever believe your own B.S."

With any degree of success, you will find a group of people that will approach you and tell you how great you are, or how smart you are, or how pretty you are. It is very flattering.

However, it begins to create a wall of stupidity in most of us. While we are slogging through disappointments and trials, we work hard to do better. Many folks confuse the aspects of doing better with being better.

NONE of us are better than anyone else. Surely each of us has talents that are not shared with our compatriots, but they have talents and abilities that we may not possess.

Egocentric people cause me a pain in the deep lower back. They tend to become so full of themselves that they treat those around them like servants or "the poor, huddled masses." Egocentric people believe they are the only ones with answers. Egocentric people think they know what everyone else needs to be doing and they take great offense when we "poor, dumb ants" don't follow their lead.

Unfortunately, many of these individuals move up the tribal ladder to positions of power and authority. That is primarily because they were helped by other people who saw something good in them.

However, once they are in those positions of power, or perceived power, they promptly forget who helped them get there. Those helpers are soon relegated to placement back in the ant hill

33

with the other poor dumb ants. If you are one of these "elitists" who actually does believe you are better than everyone else, I have a word of advice: Don't let us poor dumb ants become aware of it, because we will bite you and bite you very hard.

Understand, I don't think there is anything wrong with having a good self-image. I don't think there is anything wrong with a truthful self-evaluation of your strong points. That is called "Esteemic Value" and is in fact necessary for us to understand our position in the world, particularly if we are engaged in changing it.

The difference between Ego and Esteemic Value may be defined as this: Esteemic Value allows us to understand how we can bend our goals and ambitions in order to be successful in our endeavors. Ego is trying to determine how to bend the universe to our own wishes.

Through my studies, I became aware of the similarities between people who violate the Rule of Ego and those personalities that are described as having Antisocial Personality Disorder.

The following quotes are excerpts from an article called "Disorder: A Case of Diagnostic Confusion Psychopathy and Antisocial Personality," by Robert D. Hare, Ph.D. It was published in the 2003 *"Psychiatric Times":*

"... characteristics referred to as antisocial personality in the FBI report were as follows: sense of entitlement, unremorseful, pathetic to others, unconscionable, blameful of others, manipulative and conning, affectively cold, disparate understanding of behavior and socially acceptable behavior, disregardful of social obligations, nonconforming to social norms, irresponsible. These killers were not simply persistently antisocial individuals who met DSM-IV criteria for ASPD; they were psychopaths—remorseless predators who use charm, intimidation and, if necessary, impulsive and cold-blooded violence to attain their ends."

"Further, ASPD is very common in criminal populations, and those with the disorder are heterogeneous with respect to personality, attitudes and motivations for engaging in criminal behavior."

"The differences between psychopathy and ASPD are further highlighted by recent laboratory research involving the processing and use of linguistic and emotional information. Psychopaths differ dramatically from nonpsychopaths in their performance of a variety of cognitive and affective tasks. Compared with normal individuals, for example, psychopaths are less able to process or use the deep semantic meanings of language and to appreciate the emotional significance of events or experiences (Larbig and others; Patrick; Williamson and others)."

This is all entirely too clinical for a book such as this, so let me simplify it. Maya Angelou once said, "When someone shows you what they are the first time, believe them."

Egotists and elitists may be psychopathic, may suffer from Antisocial Personality Disorder, or they may just be jackasses.

They have the power to upset us, to anger us and to hurt us; BUT only when we give them that power.

Remember this martial arts adage, "You can't hurt what you can't hit." We can't change the wind, but we can take our sails out of it. Or we can move our sail to help use the wind more effectively. Or we can just use the wind to fly a kite. It's up to you!

Anderson's Thought

If you believe you are a god among ants, don't tell the ants. They won't like it and they will bite you!

35

RULE 11

Puppy breath does not smell good to everyone.

I believe that one of the most wonderful aromas in the world is puppy breath. It instantly gives me warm and wonderful feelings. Often I will see a puppy, pick him up and thrill its owner with my praises of what a wonderful pup he is. All I'm really doing is getting the puppy to lick my nose so I can get a dose of puppy breath. It will immediately blow a bad mood out of my head.

I love popcorn. I love the texture, I love the crunch. I consider popcorn, pizza and hamburgers to be three of the major food groups. Only twice have I gone to a movie and not purchased popcorn; both movies sucked. There is magic in popcorn.

I don't know who first made banana pudding, as that has been lost to history. I will say that the individual, whoever it was, should have been awarded the Nobel Peace Prize. I absolutely can't maintain a bad mood or anger when eating banana pudding. It is impossible. My Mom makes the world's best banana pudding.

Now, why do I mention this in this book? Simple, as I have said, we are simply individuals. Each of us has our own likes and dislikes, our own friends and enemies, treasure and trash, goods and bads.

The differences in people are what make this life so interesting. I admit, I don't understand how anyone could not like banana pudding or why some folks don't eat popcorn. I can't imagine anything sweeter than a puppy excitedly licking my nose and giving me a hit of puppy breath, but I know there are folks out there that don't like any of these things.

I know some folks that don't care for one of the three, but I refuse to keep anyone in my personal universe that doesn't like all three. I'm not saying it makes them bad people, it just means we have little in common. As I'll discuss later in the book—"like attracts like." This simply means that we like to do things with people that we have things in common with and share similar views with.

The joy of puppy breath, popcorn or banana pudding can't be explained—you have to experience them. You either get it or you don't. When you mention any of them to a stranger and they grin, that person should be seriously considered for friendship. They know how to have fun with simple things and I'll bet you can trust them.

Luckily, the good Lord has put an unending supply of puppy breath in the world, and I appreciate it. I'll share my popcorn with my wife, mom, some selected friends and even my dogs. But when it comes to banana pudding, you better be one of my grandkids or you don't even get to lick the bowl.

Anderson's Thought

There are differences in people and the differences are usually pretty good.

That is why society is made up of people, not a person. How boring to be all alike.

RULE 12

Not everyone can or wants to play in our sandbox.

One of my best friends and one of the best guys I know is a fellow named Jim Singleton; a former First Sergeant and retired Chief Master Sergeant from the Air Force Reserve.

More times than I care to admit, Jim has been my confidant and sounding board. We don't always see eye to eye, but we have always resolved the problems we have faced.

During a particularly troubling time in my life I called Jim, looking for some advice. I was frustrated by the unfairness of the world, troubled by people in responsible positions acting irresponsibly—without honor and integrity. It was so painfully simple to me what the problems were and what the solutions were. Jim agreed.

Then he said something I have never forgotten. As I said, the best truths are simple truths and they are generally short. Jim's response to my tirade that day was, "Not everyone can or wants to play in our sandbox."

My response to him was, "'Nuff said, thanks Top!"

I don't understand why someone would not want to "play in our sandbox," but I realized Jim was right. Some kids can work well with others and have fun in the sandbox. Some kids want to rule the sandbox; and some kids just want to kick the sand out of the sandbox because for them, that's fun.

Some folks never grow out of that.

Anderson's Thought

Every person has something to teach you. Some show you what to be and what to do.

Others are just good examples of bad examples. We can learn from both.

RULE 13

The things that are important to me only have to be important to me.

Long ago, I realized that I march to the beat of a different drummer. Recently, I found there are a lot of other silent marchers in my parade. These folks have often been described as "the silent majority."

There are folks who are busy making a living, raising their kids, loving their wives, honoring the flag and trying to face the obstacles and challenges that life places in front of them. The method they use is considered by many to be old fashioned. It is called hard work.

These folks consider a higher power to be God, not the government. They figure the source of their strength is the power of their convictions, commitments and their belief in their God. They pray quietly. They serve gallantly. At the end of their day, their reward is to go home and enjoy their families.

As young adult, I was often embarrassed by my father's tears. I remember the first time I saw him cry. Our dog Bozo had died and it made sense for the tears to flow.

The next time was the day I was leaving for college. It was the biggest day of my life. It was what I had worked for all of my years in school and my old man had tears in his eyes. I could not imagine what was wrong with him. I could not imagine until I had kids and it was their time to move out. Then I understood but by then, as often happens, it was too late to tell Dad I finally understood.

I feel an undesirable swelling of pride and humility when I hear the national anthem. I feel a sense of belonging and gratitude when I see our flag wave. I feel a sense of dread and anxiety when I watch the news, and see our service men and women in foreign countries serving our country in harm's way.

I love saluting and the sound of Taps being played in ripple. I love the Missing Man formation when it is performed, and I hate that it has to be performed.

I love seeing a service person walking when their uniform is straight away and their appearance shows their pride without speaking. I love to see old veterans and their wives stand for the national anthem, even when the idiots around them don't.

I love that I had the honor of throwing the first pitch with my Wing Commander at the first Astros home game after September 11, 2001. I loved the patriotism and support shown by thousands of people as they chanted U.S.A., U.S.A.!

I love that I met President George W. Bush and he returned my salute. I love that I've been to the Pentagon and found a five-acre park in the dead center of the structure. I love that I got to meet one of my heroes, Bob Gaylor, Fifth Chief Master Sergeant of the Air Force, and we became friends.

I love that I have been to our nation's capital where I saw The Wall and had a "drink" with the folks memorialized on it. I love that I have served with some of the best Americans that ever lived. I love that I served with some of the worst; they showed me what not to do.

I have many loves.

I love the feel of a single action revolver in my hand. I love it when that same hand is filled by the smaller hands of my grandkids when we go walking. I love cool weather and the mountains. I love old music, not the noise of today.

I love the sense of flying that downhill skiing gives. I love the freedom of being on a motorcycle.

I love the feel of a good horse under me and the sense of completion of having a good dog at my feet. I love the lines of a fine made knife. I love the feeling of accomplishment when I have put a good edge on that knife.

I love a good joke, even if it may be politically incorrect. I love a military drill team's performance. I love old places and old things; I remember when they were new.

I love the smell of a baseball glove. No other piece of leather has the same smell. I love the slap of the ball when it slams into the glove. I love the monotony of a game of pitch. I love the excitement of a ball game and the utter peace of watching the ocean, a tumbling brook or rippling stream or a bird in flight.

I love the little gifts that God has given me—like on my first parachute jump when I looked below me and saw the top of a hawk circling beneath me. Wow!

I love the smell of gunpowder and the accomplishment of a good group of hits on the target. I love the Lone Ranger, Clayton Moore that is. I love it when the underdog wins.

I love the Alamo in San Antonio, and I love the one in Brackettville, Texas. I have been to both many times. I revere the one in San Antonio but in the one in Brackettville, I have stood where the Duke stood, I have spat where the Duke spat and I have peed where the Duke peed.

Not bad, not bad at all.

I love that I have good friends and worthy enemies. I love that I have a sense of history. I love that I enjoy writing and speaking to folks. I love that my country is free. I love that we have the freedom to speak our minds, even though I don't always agree with some of my countrymen.

I love old Star Trek episodes and the new ones. I love that I have lived to see Superman, Batman, Spiderman and Daredevil on the silver screen. Their lessons might be lost on a new generation if these folks see just the special effects.

I love that I had the opportunity to speak to Roy Rogers on 21 November, 1991. I love that I know who Gene Autry and Rocky Lane were. I love that Tom Mix cried at Wyatt Earp's funeral.

I love that my son has grown up to be a good father, a good man, and a good son. I love that my daughter is a wonderful mother, a good woman and a good daughter.

I love that they have made mistakes but have not been defined by those mistakes. I love that they did not always listen to me; instead they listened to their own wisdom and made good lives. I love that my grandkids will learn by watching them.

I love that I have a brother, although we don't always understand each other. We don't have to, we're brothers.

I love that I still have my Mom; I am just now starting to meet her. I wish that I knew more about my Dad's service to my country, but I understand why he didn't talk about it.

I love that I was raised in a family where all of my uncles and my father fought in and survived World War II. I love that the guy that taught me to be a sergeant was my Dad. I love that my Mom taught me to write; little did she realize what she was starting.

I love that I was born in Texas. I love that I cry every time I see "Ol' Yeller." I love that I remember life before television. I remember when all phones looked alike; they were black and had dials. I remember when I did not have a cell phone, a computer and when I saw my first bottle of White Out—now that was good stuff! I love that I got to interview John Scopes when I was in college; he was the defendant in the Monkey Trial.

I love that I went to Woodlawn High School. We were called the Knights, so naturally we called our school the Castle. For us, Camelot was real. I love that I know about King Arthur and the Roundtable and that I learned Merlin was the real hero of the story.

I love Fanner 50's and Greenie Stick-um caps and Shootin' Shells and Icees and banana splits and Butterfingers and Zero candy bars. I love Trigger and Bullet and Champion and Topper and Fury, and all other beautiful and heroic horses and dogs.

I love that I had Lady, Dash, Rusty, Bozo, Beau Diddley, Princess, Frisky, Cargo, Buddha, Muffin, Jack Daniels and Gibson— better dogs never lived; that is with the possible exceptions of Annie and Taffy, our current canine companions.

I love that I had a cat named Tink and another cat named Tink. I don't like cats, but I have loved these.

I love that in my darkest times, God saw fit to make me live through them and prosper. I love that I have had wonderful women in my life to show me the errors of my ways and help me learn to be a man.

I love that I found who I was looking for all of those years. She allows me to be a dad, a granddad and to have served my country. She makes me better than I ever would be alone. I love that she wanted what I was selling.

None of these things will alter the rotation of the earth. None of these things will change the universe. None of these things have a particular meaning to anyone other than me. That's okay, that is the way it is supposed to be and it's more than enough for me.

Anderson's Thought

The world is full of joys and blessings that most folks don't see, but that is just because they aren't looking!

RULE 14

Success is finding someone who wants what you're selling.

Our society has missed a couple of points in the processing of information. There are books out on how to manipulate someone, how to confuse the issues and how to talk around the subject. All of these are designed to "teach someone how to sell."

I think we are missing the boat. I think what we need to be focused on is how to make something that someone wants to buy. Now that may be a subtle difference for some folks, but it is a significant one for me.

It is a rule of economics that if you make a good product and offer that product at a fair price, someone will want to buy it; and when they need another, they will buy it again. It is also a rule of economics that if you make a bad product or offer that product at an unfair price, you might convince some folks to buy it—once.

This holds true also when you are dealing with people and relationships. I know folks that are like willows in the wind. They are chameleons; they will be whatever the person they are with wants them to be. Change the person they are with and their demeanor, personality and ethics seem to change to fit that set of circumstances.

Country western singer George Strait has a song that says, "Well, excuse me, but I think you've got my chair." This was his opening line to an unknown young lady. During the song, the relationship develops and she leaves with him at the end; but the last line of the song says, "By the way, that wasn't my chair after all."

In most human endeavors we relate like salesmen, not craftsman. We try to trick someone else into believing "we" are the kind of person they want. This is a process that can work for a limited period of time—occasionally.

Once that period of time has elapsed, be it hours, days, weeks or months, the "buyer" realizes they were sold a bill of goods and the "seller" is frustrated because the "deal" fell through.

I was as guilty of this as anyone else. One day I realized that I could not "sell" me if I did not know who I was, what I believed in, and what I stood for. Once I figured those things out, once I became honest with myself and those around me, a very interesting thing occurred. I proved the first law of economics. Once I decided to really be myself, someone decided they wanted me—the way I was. Not the way they wanted to make me, not the way they wanted to see me but the way I was.

That was, and still is, the secret of success. I stopped trying to "sell" myself and began enjoying being "purchased and appreciated" because the customer "bought" exactly what they wanted. It makes all of the difference in the world.

Anderson's Thought

"Like attracts like."
                    Illusion—The Adventures of a Reluctant Messiah
                                        —Richard Bach

RULE 15

Be a lightening bug.

As a professional speaker, I have studied other speakers to see how they do what we do. I am always fascinated by the latest buzz program or techniques that are taught. But remember, "All thoughts that can be thought have been thought—I think."

So, in other words, each of us is simply recycling thoughts that someone else came up with and we change it a little for our own techniques and programs.

How to find a lasting relationship is often in the list of questions that are asked of me, following my program on Relationships and Communications.

Certainly today's world is troubled, and the life of any relationship is at best dubious. Yet, we still hear success stories of wonderful friendships, true love and lasting love. I like simple truths and this is one of the best analogies I have ever heard.

Most relationships begin by both parties trying to put their best foot forward. Most begin by both parties trying to determine what the other person wants to hear and then demonstrating those behaviors or attributes. Inevitably, the excitement of the first meetings begin to fade and we all must settle into the seemingly boring aspects of just being who we really are.

Now, if we are trying to put our best foot forward and we are trying to demonstrate what our partners want, why do fifty percent of first marriages and eighty percent of second marriages fail? It's this simple: We try to be what we think someone else wants, not who and what we really are.

Have you ever seen a lightening bug or fire fly on a summer evening? At first, there is usually only one. He doesn't fly around shouting, "Hey Baby, you're beautiful, I'm sensitive!" "What's your sign? Really? Me too!" "I can make you happy. I will make you happy." "I will respect you always."

Nope, he just flies around and blinks his little light. Pretty soon, other fire flies begin to appear. All he does is blink his light to show them what he is and where he is and the others come to that light.

If people would only learn: be who you really are, not what you think someone else wants.

Someone is looking for exactly who you are—they will find you if you just demonstrate it. Talk is cheap and actions speak louder than words. Just shine your light.

Success is finding someone who wants what you're selling. You don't have to trick anyone. Verbal judo will get you in trouble. The latest lines don't work. Sure you can trick someone into believing that you are Prince Charming; but if you are not, that armor is going to get very heavy after a while and you'll need to shine it regularly.

Insensitive people can only fake sensitivity for so long. Cat haters rarely learn to love cats. How many tractor pulls can you go to if you don't really like them?

Rodeos don't make sense, tractor pulls are just loud, car shows are boring and antiques are just old junk unless you like them. You develop friends because they like the same things that you do. However, we seem to pick spouses for different reasons.

Now I am not saying that we should not have friends. I am saying spouses work better when you have something in common besides children, sex and troubled finances.

One day I stopped trying to be what someone else wanted me to be. I decided who I wanted to be and set out on that journey.

Just a few steps down the road, I found someone who wanted what I was.

Now I have to admit, from time to time, Pam's little "change monster" rears its ugly head, but that's alright. That is part of the wonder of women.

They are change agents. They are the civilizers. Left to our own devices, most men could care less about the color of curtains or even if there are curtains. Women get fed up with the world that exists and tell their men to change it.

There's nothing wrong with changing the world but remember, we can't change anyone else. If you are in a relationship because you think you will eventually change that person into what you want—you are wrong and the relationship is doomed.

First of all, figure out who you are. Second, be that person. Third, get ready, there is someone out there looking for you. If you are honest and they are honest, it will work.

My son sent me an email a few years ago. It had a picture of a drop dead beautiful, buxom young lady in a bikini. On a scale of one to ten for looks, she was a twelve; but below her picture were instructions to scroll down.

Like a great comedian, the email made you wait for the final word. After a minute of watching the scroll down marks there was a box with the following message: "Somewhere there is a man who is tired of her crap."

Don't find someone who looks like what you want. Find someone who likes what you are. It makes all the difference. There is an additional aspect to this philosophy; it is called Like Attracts Like. This again comes from the book *Illusions*.

Richard Bach identified that we have friends with whom we share a lot of similarities. We are by no means identical but we share the same passions, hate the same things, and love the same things.

Anderson's Rules

Each of us is free to live our lives according to our own rules; but MOST important of all, we can talk to each other and try to understand what the other person is talking about and feeling.

I have met folks that I instantly recognized as being like me. Those folks tend to stay in my life. The strange thing is we may not speak for months or years yet, when we do speak, we are able to pick up right where we left off in the last conversation. It is a magical thing that I treasure.

Some folks come into my life and make a "deposit" then leave. Sometimes this deposit is a treasure and sometimes it is a bucket of manure. It depends on the person and how closely I examine the gift. The treasures are always nice and I enjoy them.

Sometimes the bucket is full of stuff that I don't want but I need. Remember the sweetest flowers need fertilizer to grow. I'll talk more about that when I discuss the importance of sharpening a knife and how it relates to life.

Right now I want to talk about the treasures—ahh, the treasures. Most are usually small things, wondrous things. They are things I like. They are things that my friends like also. That is the joy of it all. When my friends and I talk, we talk about things we like. When my friends and I do something, we do something we both like.

We don't try to change each other. When we laugh it is because we both understand the joke. When we cry, it is because we both feel the pain. It is not easy being a friend to me or my friends and yet it is painfully simple. Say what you mean and do what you say.

I have also examined my loves. I discovered that opposites may attract but they don't stick—at least not for long. The dynamics of such relationships are hard and will wear you down and wear you out. It's not fun and it's hard. It's not impossible, but definitely hard.

51

Think about it, why would you want to spend time with some-one you don't have anything in common with? In time, people figure out the answer to this question. The answer is they don't, and then you end up with divorce. Informal relationships without commonalities as a basis of the relationship, also fail.

I found that the best relationship I ever had was with a friend. We had the same passions, the same hates, the same loves, the same goals, and the same level of commitments.

So I married her and as the story goes, the rest is history—a very good history. Not only is she my wife, she is my friend. I have to live up to her expectations of me and that has made me better. We both strive to be better people than we would ever have been without the other.

Like attracts like.

Anderson's Thought

What is—is. Therefore, what ain't—ain't. And it is what it is till it ain't that no more. Usually it is you that has to change it.

Get that; it is important!

RULE 16

Love is saying you're sorry and meaning it.

When the movie *Love Story* came out, the message was "Love is never having to say you're sorry." It is a wonderful concept but I kept screwing up this "Love" thing. It was not on purpose, it just kept happening. I would not realize until much later that most of the problems I experienced with love were my own fault.

I would eventually learn that no one could come up to my expectations and I could not come up to someone else's expectations, if those expectations were not known. Also, those expectations had to be agreed on; and if that agreement was not forthcoming, the expectations had to be negotiated to a different level.

This is just one of many aspects of living and loving I would discover. On the third try at marriage, I got it right; but that can't be credited to me. Yet, even in this relationship, I found that challenges still existed and problems would create havoc and turmoil if they were allowed to. I had found someone that:

a) wanted what I was selling

b) did not want to change me

c) I could look up to

Yet problems still occurred. The main reason for that is simple—she is a woman and I am a man. We do not think alike. We process information differently. We have different expectations. We communicate differently.

There have been times when we both have had to say we're sorry. I guess the big difference is—we meant it. We were sorry.

53

We wanted this relationship to work. We had seen success and we believed we could be successful and that we were worth it. We decided we wanted to be with each other more than anything else. It really isn't that hard when you have the right tools.

I struggled because my tools were "American Standard" and then I found my problems were "Metric." I had to change my view of what the problems were. I was lucky, I made that change. I was saved.

I realized Pam was not trying to change me, she was trying to improve me. She was refining me, not defining me. I also realized that there were only three issues we ever fought about.

The first was her family of origin issues. The second was her giving me unwanted advice and criticism, and the last occurred when we failed to adequately describe our expectations or agree on them.

I realized that it was not sufficient for either of us to say we were sorry. It was essential that we develop a plan to prevent the problem from reoccurring. Say you're sorry, but show what change in behavior you are going to make in order to keep it from happening again.

It's called accountability. That's right, you have to respect your spouse and be accountable to him or her.

I realized that we both had not only a right but an obligation to stand up for what we believed. Because my wife is a pretty sharp lady, one of her greatest qualities is she hates to fight. That is not to say she is unwilling to fight, that would denote a lack of courage. She prefers resolution to revolution.

I fight. Sometimes, I have to admit, I kind of like it. I am used to it because of past relationships and I grew to expect a fight. Pam does not fight. Once I realized that I did not have to fight and that we could negotiate, the fighting stopped.

Occasionally, it is necessary to revisit issues. Occasionally, it is necessary to "beat this dog some more." Sometimes that is because I see behavior in her that triggers my old "fight or flight" reactions.

Sometimes I am right. Sometimes I just need to understand where her head is at that moment. I know where her heart is. Luckily, I have someone that is good at talking and listening, someone who does not want to fight.

Luckily, she is smarter than me in a lot of areas. We each have our areas of expertise, where we are subject matter experts. We don't compete with each other and we don't compromise. I've heard it said that compromise is an Italian word that means both people get screwed.

We compensate. That means we do not play games. We don't barter each other's emotional reactions. We do something not because the other person wants us to, but because we want the other person to enjoy what we've done.

Yes, we actually like to please one another. What a concept! I get pleasure out of giving her pleasure.

Anderson's Thought

Love is an emotion affirmed by actions.

RULE 17

If you can't shoot your own dog, get out of the business.

For years I have used the analogy of "Ol' Yeller" to teach supervisors and managers how to supervise and manage. However, I've come to realize from my recent presentations on leadership, it's not just for managers and supervisors.

It's a lesson that each of us can use in our daily lives and in our personal relationships. I've received overwhelming response to the concept that doing the right things usually means doing the hard things. Sometimes this shows up as "Leadership by Example." The important thing to remember is this: It is just as important in our personal life as it is in our professional one. Here is the story of 'Ol Yeller:

'Ol Yeller—by Fred Gipson and Walt Disney

It was in the 1840s, down in the Texas hill country when the story took place. On a small farm, a family of four had struggled against Indians, weather, and hardship to make a life. The father leaves for a three month cattle drive along with the other men in the loosely structured community. His oldest son, Travis, is left to be "the man of the house" in his father's absence.

After the father was gone for a couple of days, a yellow mongrel dog shows up and decides to "adopt the family."

Artis, Travis' brother, loves the dog and begs his older brother to let the dog stay. Begrudgingly, Travis allows the dog to stay. Over the next weeks, the dog becomes a valued pet and even Travis feels a bond with the dog. They named him Yeller.

One day Travis and Yeller are out in the woods when they are suddenly attacked by wild hogs. Yeller valiantly defends Travis, saving his life. Yeller is seriously injured and Travis, wounded himself, goes for help.

Treated by his mother, Travis refuses to abandon Yeller and insists on going back to get him. With great difficulty, Yeller is brought home and successfully treated. Yeller is fully accepted as part of the family now.

Then neighbors send word of an outbreak of rabies in the area. Travis and his mother realize one of their cows is infected. Travis shoots the cow and they decide to cremate the body to prevent spread of the disease.

Travis' injuries prevent him from hauling wood, so the mother and a young neighbor girl haul wood and build a bonfire. They continue to haul wood in order to keep the fire going until the body has been consumed.

Suddenly, Travis hears his mother scream for help; Travis grabs his rifle and hobbles to the scene. Travis can see by the light of the bonfire that Yeller and a wolf are locked in deadly combat. Travis takes aim and fires, killing the wolf. His mother explains that the wolf attacked and Yeller saved them.

Travis feels very proud that Yeller is a hero again. Then the mother realizes, "No sane wolf would attack this close to the fire." She suspects the wolf is infected with rabies.

When Travis' mother tells him this and she asks him to shoot Yeller, the boy is devastated. Travis convinces his mother to let him pen up the dog to see if the symptoms of rabies would develop.

After being penned up for a while, Yeller is apparently healthy and Artis forces the issue to let Yeller out. He opens the door to the pen and slams it shut. Yeller snarls and is foaming at the mouth. He has rabies.

Travis is devastated because now there are no other options. He must act. If he does not act, his friend will suffer a horrible and lengthy death. If he does not act, Yeller could escape and attack a family member or friend.

Travis' mother offers to shoot Yeller but Travis says, "No, he's my dog. I'll do it."

In that terrible moment, Travis chose to do a hard thing because it was the right thing to do. While it was not a conscious thing, he demonstrated leadership by example to his younger brother.

In the days and weeks following this terrible incident, Travis chooses to have a positive attitude. He honored Yeller's memory and gathered strength and character from the ordeal.

This is what a leader does. Now, let's look at the similarities found in this story and how they correlate to leadership. Travis demonstrated good decision making and reasoning when he convinces his mother to let him pen up Yeller. In any tough dilemma, if time allows, we should evaluate the problem before we take action that can't be undone.

When it's determined that Yeller does in fact have rabies, Travis chooses to "hire himself to manage himself" and be accountable and responsible. These are qualities and characteristics that we should use in any dilemma or professional difficulty.

Let's look at this also in terms of personal relationships. Have you ever had to end a relationship with someone that you knew was not good for you? Or, maybe you knew you should end it but didn't have the guts to do so.

What is the answer? Simple—hire yourself to manage yourself. Do as good a job for yourself as you would for an employer.

Give yourself the same good advice you would give your best friend.

We are all either followers or leaders, and we change periodically and episodically in those roles depending on circumstance.

Do you know how people view you? Do people respect you and ask for your advice? Do you listen to what others say and incorporate their ideas to make yourself a better person? Do people take your advice?

Remember, just because you are a manager or supervisor does not mean you are viewed by others as a leader. Do you stand up for what is right or are you a "yes" man or woman?

Look again at the title of this section. It does not say, "Do you want to shoot your own dog?" No one wants to have to do that. It reads, "Can you shoot your own dog?"

Can you do the hard things that you do not want to do?

Can you take the right path when it is not the easiest path?

Can you do the right thing when it is unpopular?

Can you do your duty even when doing that duty places you in opposition to your friends and colleagues?

Can you do the hard and right things that you do not want to do?

Can you shoot your own dog?

Anderson's Thought

Doing hard things requires courage and the ability to see past our own fears, failings and feelings.

It is therefore for the greater good, not our comfort, that we must do hard things.

RULE 18

A "sphincterectomy" is required every couple of years.

Several years ago, I became aware that I attract two types of people. Some are very strong personalities and these people are generally fun to be with because we don't intimidate each other. Others are weaker and sometimes it is hard to tell the difference in the beginning.

Then as time goes on, the weaker ones want me to "fix" them and I can't. They want me to alter their universe so their problems go away, so they can be more successful and more fulfilled.

Some of these will listen and take advice and guidance but I can't "fix" them. Only they can "fix" themselves. Most don't really want to be fixed or they would already be fixed. These are people that need DRAMA in their lives to know they are alive. They can, and do, continue to make decisions that create chaos in their lives. This chaos is what I call DRAMA and I call these people "the daytime soap opera people."

They will not fix their lives because they would not be able to define their own existence without the DRAMA. Unfortunately, they are usually pretty interesting folks with a tremendous amount of potential. They could be so great, if only...

These are the folks I referred to earlier in Anderson's Rule of Large Numbers. These folks are in that last two percent. They have chosen to be who and what they are and nothing will change that until, and if, they become ready to change—and most never will change.

In the meantime, they suck your soul out. They cost you tremendously in emotional turmoil and uproar.

As I said, sometimes these people are hard to identify because they are so close to the three percent that can become the elite. I have yet to define what characteristics are different in the two percenters and the three percenters. I wish I could; it would save us all a lot of wear and tear but I haven't figured it out yet.

Therefore, every couple of years, I have to examine the folks I have allowed in my life and make a determination to "cut some a------s out." Otherwise, I lose my own direction trying to effect change in people that have chosen not to change.

I recommend the same procedure to you. It is not easy and sometimes it means cutting folks out of your life that you have given a lot of value to. But if you don't do it, you will become like them and that is unacceptable. This is a great example of shooting your own dog!

Anderson's Thought

Only spend your energy on people that want to be the best they can be.

Everyone will tell you what they "can do"; your job is to evaluate what they are "doing."

RULE 19

Changing opinion is like playing on the merry-go-round.

Many years ago, when I first became involved with law enforcement, I was honored by being named the head of a new project. After about a month in the job, I realized that many of the problems that I was facing should have already been fixed but were not.

This troubled me. While I was a good cop and not a dumb person, I knew that there were people that were far better cops than I would ever be and far smarter than I could ever hope to be, who had come and gone before me.

Why had they not "fixed" these problems? A month later, I came to what I thought was the answer—no one wanted it fixed. In reality it was only half the answer. Years later I stumbled on the second part of the answer—it can't be fixed.

We, as human beings, must constantly relearn ultimate truths. Most bureaucracies exist for the sole purpose of perpetuating themselves. Therefore, these bureaucracies do not want things "fixed." If they get "fixed," the members of the bureaucracy find that they are no longer needed. It is far better for a bureaucracy to continually shift attention from problem to problem than it is to fix that problem.

This process is cyclical. New people try to fix old problems but most of the time it doesn't work. They are simply trying to "re-fix" what is broken by "throwing stuff" at the problem or "doing things" that only serve as insignificant and temporary bandages for serious problems. In that manner, the bureaucracies get to continue to function.

I am reminded of Will Rogers' statement, "There are three kinds of learners in the world. There are those that learn by watching other people make mistakes. There are those that can read about others making mistakes and learn. Then there are those that just have to urinate on the hot wire."

Unfortunately, most adults fall into the last category. If you have children that are now adults, you know that even with all of the guidance and direction that you provided as a parent, they still make many some of the same mistakes that you did. Wouldn't it be wonderful if the parents could make the mistakes and keep their children from stepping on those landmines?

However, those children must also learn for themselves. They must experience the aspects of failure, humiliation and mistake-making before they can incorporate the tasks involved with good judgment and problem solving.

One of my favorite quotes is again from Will Rogers. "Good judgment comes from experience and most good experience comes from bad judgment."

I remember when I was a kid I loved the merry-go-round; but if you got there before everyone else, it was really hard to get it started. Once it was moving and gained speed, it was easier to push, particularly if you had help. With enough help, it finally got to a point where one kid could stand alongside and just slap the handles as they went by and it would keep going.

That's sort of like changing opinions. It is hard at first. It works better if you have help; and once it's moving, someone has to miss the ride so everyone else can enjoy it. Keep slapping those handles.

But it helps also to remember that opinions are like noses—everyone has one and most of them smell.

Bob Anderson

Anderson's Thought

Remember, don't give to malice what stupidity should own.

RULE 20

Don't confuse activity with accomplishment.

Years ago, I found that muscle soreness goes away in seven days if you keep exercising. If you quit, it goes away in a week. A cold goes away in seven days if you take medicine. It leaves in a week if you don't.

I think we have become too fascinated with technology and addicted to immediate gratification. As Americans, we want an immediate fix.

We want to take an action that gives us immediate satisfaction and makes us feel good. Most of the time, we do not spend the time to determine if it makes any difference at all in the long run.

Several years ago, I lived in a town in northwest Louisiana. There was a lot of construction being done on the interstate. I got frustrated with sitting in traffic. From where the road block was, it took almost forty minutes to get through the traffic jam and back to my home. One day I "broke out of the herd."

I took a side road and after traveling through the "back way," I got home. That trip took forty minutes.

Then I realized that at the road block, I was sitting still for long periods of time, moving at a top speed of ten miles per hour with one-way traffic going the same direction as me. It took forty minutes and was safer.

It was safer than moving through multiple intersections with all possible traffic patterns, traveling a speed in excess of forty miles per hour. It just felt better; I was busy and I was in motion.

Americans seem to have a problem with sitting still. Many of us feel that we must be in motion, even if that motion puts us at higher risk with no increase in reward.

Don't confuse activity with accomplishment. I know many people that are "busy" throughout their entire work day. They are active! However, their productivity is usually far less than their counterparts who have a plan and use their energy toward production rather than public relations. IF they would "produce" instead of "excuse," they would be successful.

If THEY worked hard at what THEY were supposed to be working at instead of what THEY had decided was their job, THEY would be successful. If THEY would work hard at what THEY are supposed to be working at, instead of creating explanations as to why they could not complete their tasks, THEY would be successful. But THEY won't.

If you work correctly at what you are supposed to do and complete tasks, you will intimidate those around you that do not. If you do, you will find legions of people who will attack you but you will also be successful.

Why? Because your success will not be because you are that good; it is because everyone else really is that bad.

Anderson's Thought

Sometimes, there is no answer to a question. You just have to live through it.

RULE 21

Your success is not because you are that good; it's because everyone else really is that bad.

Over the past fifteen years, I have conducted an unofficial study of successful people. I will now share the results of that study with you. Without exception, those successful people I have visited with share one thing in common. They have exceeded the performance of their peers without straining.

That's correct. Not a single one was able to point to something they have accomplished that really strained them. This world has become so used to "good enough" and "close enough for government work," that excellence seems to be a dying commodity.

These people did, however, share a good work ethic. They returned phone calls and emails in a timely fashion. They said what they meant and they did what they said.

These qualities, more so than education, experience or any other quantifiable characteristic, are what they share. With little more in common, these people came from all walks of life and many different types of companies and some were in the military.

Now, I must point out that almost all of them share something else. Many people found them intimidating. After a lot of research into this characteristic, I have come to a conclusion. If you are competent and you are confident, you will intimidate those around you who are less of either, and there is little you can do about it except disguise your competence and your confidence.

There was a book that came out in the seventies titled, *I'm Okay, You're Okay.* Well I have taken the liberty to expand that concept. It is my opinion that "I'm okay, you're okay—they're screwed up." Thank goodness!

Anderson's Thought

My success or my failure is my responsibility.

RULE 22

Never give to malice what stupidity should own.

I have to admit that I suffer from a couple of maladies. I tend to expect folks to honor what they say. I tend to expect folks to do what they say they are going to do. I tend to be somewhat paranoid but I also adhere to the concept that, "Just because you're paranoid doesn't mean they are not after you."

I discovered several years ago that people will try to destroy you. Not because they don't like you; some of my best friends became my worst enemies. I learned that some of the worst attacks I have ever received were not based on malice. These folks did not want to hurt me, even though they did. These folks did not want to invalidate me, even though they did. Some folks just don't see things the way that I do.

Generally speaking, I've found it difficult to sell training programs that have concepts of accountability and responsibility built into the curriculum. This is particularly true for organizations whose problems are based on the facts that they have no accountability and do not require their folks to be responsible.

Originally, I thought the problem was simple—no one was being held to account and no one knew who to be responsible to.

Originally, when I ran into problems teaching such programs, I thought it was based on malice. I thought that people became obstacles because they did not like me or did not believe in the programs.

Subsequently, I realized that these individuals just did not want the problems solved because:

1) it would mean the end of a bureaucracy

2) it would mean extra work

3) it would mean someone else would be watching and evaluating them

The fact that the solution for most business issues is to implement a consistent program of accountability and responsibility wasn't tremendously relevant.

THEY would prefer a healthy organization to stumble and die than do what was necessary to save it. That is stupidity!

Someone in Texas once said, "Ignorant people can be fixed by education, but stupid goes clean to the bone."

Another of my favorite quotes from Shakespeare says, "No man thinks himself a scoundrel." This is absolutely accurate. People with no integrity are masters at justifying their behavior.

People with situational ethics have made "explanation of the unexplainable" into an art form. In psychological terms, this could be called psychopathic behavior. In its extreme criminal patterns, it is recognizable.

In a polite society, it is more difficult to identify. The unscrupulous politician can "explain" why he did not keep his campaign promises. The unethical businessman can "explain" why he violated the trust of his stockholders and employees. The cheating husband can always "blame" his wife's behavior for his wrong behavior. The captured criminal can always "blame" society for his actions.

This process is not new in human experience. We, as a society, want to find out why someone did something with the mistaken belief that if we can understand it, we can prevent it.

The truth is that it may be possible in some cases but it is my considered opinion that, as Buddha said, "Life is hard." Without being cynical I quote Bruce Willis' character in the movie *Last*

Boy Scout, "Water is wet, the sky is blue and Satan Claus is out there."

Since we are easily convinced that we are not scoundrels, it becomes contingent on us to evaluate our behavior for its impact on others. For every good deed, there is a negative impact for someone. For every bad deed, there is someone who prospers.

One of my old psychology instructors was fond of saying, "I will not provide you with answers to life's questions. I will simply try to give you more questions."

I can't tell you how to live your life or what decisions to make. I can tell you that "damned if you do and damned if you don't" are never equal. You have to decide what the "right" answer is and stand behind that decision. You have to determine what "good" looks like in your life.

I can tell you this: If you benefit from someone else's loss, if you don't believe in magic, if you don't believe in the innate good of man, if you don't believe in a higher power, if you prosper by preventing someone else from prospering, if you constantly win by making other people lose, if you use people to promote your own good, if you feel you're better than everyone else, if you can justify behavior that you know is wrong, if you don't keep your promises, if you are a proponent of situational ethics, if you don't honor your own word, if you blame someone else for making you do something you know is wrong, if you blame your own bad behavior on what someone else did to you—read Shakespeare, you are a scoundrel.

Anderson's Thought

Perspective is an individual opinion; change it and you change the world.

RULE 23

You have to believe in magic.

The challenge coin is a military tradition that began during World War I. Today they come in a variety of shapes, colors and designs. They can identify either specific military units or individuals. The collection of these challenge coins is an exciting and fulfilling hobby for me.

The presentation of these coins is meant to be a special and honored ritual. The proper way to present a coin is as follows: The person presenting the coin extends his/her right hand as if to shake hands. The coin is lying on that person's palm. The person receiving the coin shakes hands and the presenter turns their hands over so the coin passes to the recipient.

When I learned that I was to become the Command Chief Master Sergeant for the 147th Fighter Wing at Ellington Field, I began to design my personal coin. At that point in time, becoming Command Chief was the high point of my military career.

I wanted the coin to do many things. I wanted to identify the salient points that had moved my career to this zenith. I wanted it to identify my unit and my position. I also wanted to honor my family. It took three months to finalize the design.

Because it is unique, I have received a lot of questions concerning the symbols on this coin. On the obverse, my position and wing are identified above the chevron for the Command Chief Master Sergeant. Below the chevron is the name of my base at that time, Ellington Field. Below that is my given name, my nickname and my status as a Ph.D.

On the reverse, across the top of the coin is the question: "Can you shoot your own dog?" The meaning for this I described in a previous essay dealing with Ol' Yeller.

In the center is a blue feather. This comes from Richard Bach's book, *Illusions—The Adventures of a Reluctant Messiah*. I've mentioned it earlier. This is probably the most significant book I have ever read; and to date, I have read it fifty-nine times.

In *Illusions*, there is a description on how to "magnetize good things into your life." In the book, a blue feather was used as an illustration. Each time I have "magnetized" a blue feather, I have actually found one.

During a particularly lousy time in my life around 1988, I left my house for a five-mile jog. As I always did, I drew a line in the sand and gravel of the road and started running. This day I decided I was in serious need of some "magic" and I went through the process described in *Illusions* for magnetizing.

As I ran past the finish line, I noticed there was a feather—a blue feather lying on the line I had drawn. I went back and retrieved the feather. I had never seen one like it before. On one side, it was a beautiful deep blue; on the other side it was golden.

Three weeks later, I saw my first tropical blue Macaw. I realized the feather I found had come from such a bird. Now, I don't know what the odds are of a blue Macaw flying over northwest Louisiana on that day, at that time, and dropping a single blue feather and having it land exactly on that line; but it impressed the hell out of me. So I put some magic on that coin and added a blue feather. (If you want to learn more about this magic, I recommend you read a special book called *Sacred Feathers—The Power of One Feather to Change Your Life*, by Maril Crabtree. It contains numerous stories of feather magic. I was fortunate to be able to tell my blue feather story in this book.)

To the left of the feather is a glyph my son John designed when he first read *Lord of the Rings* by J.R.R. Tolkin. Below it are the initials SK, these are for John's daughters, my granddaughters, Sarah and Kayleigh.

To the right of the feather is a bear's head; my daughter Shelley's childhood nickname was Sugar Bear. Below it are the initials RJS, these are for Shelley's children, my granddaughter, Rachel, and my grandsons, Josh and Seth.

Next is the statement "Everything and more." One of the best officers I ever served under was my dear friend David A. Bond, COL, USAF (Ret). He has the Bond family motto, "Even the world is not enough" on his wall. I thought that was really neat and set out to come up with the Anderson motto. It became—Everything and More! That is what I want out of life.

Finally the most unusual item on the coin is the word PAROMEBELART. Now if you ask my son, he'll tell you it is Latin for "Kill them all and let God sort them out." In reality, it is my name and my wife's name intertwined.

Pamela and Robert: PA-RO-ME-BE-LA-RT

Richard Bach says, "Don't forget what you did today. It is easy to forget our times of knowing, to think they've been dreams or old miracles, one time. Nothing is a miracle, nothing lovely is a dream."

I have also mentioned King Arthur, the Knights of the Roundtable and Camelot, another magical story. There is a movie from several years ago called EXCALIBUR. It is about King Arthur. In one scene, Merlin the Magician tells Arthur and his knights that, "The problem with man is he forgets the magic he does."

I'm sure that there have been times when you pulled something off that "couldn't be done." You won a battle you should have lost. You caught a ball you should have missed. You were dead broke and found a twenty. You took a chance and it paid off.

Probably each human being encounters thousands of these "magical events" during each life time but most folks write them off as coincidences, luck or fortune.

I say: Play a little and let there be magic. Richard Bach said, "You are led through your lifetime by the inner learning creature, the playful spiritual being that is your real self. Don't turn away from possible futures before you're certain you don't have anything to learn from them. You're always free to change your mind and choose a different future, or a different past."

That last line, "You're always free to change your mind and choose a different future, or a different past," is the single most powerful line I have ever read.

I knew I was always able to affect my future but until I read that line, I had no idea I could affect my past. At that point, I realized that it was my attitude that colored what lessons, if any, came from my past.

It was my attitude that determined whether I was a victim of the past or a victor because of it.

That, my friend, is magic.

Anderson's Thought

Magic is the fingerprint of God.

RULE 24

Practice random acts of kindness.

There is a wonderful little book called *Random Acts of Kindness* by Dr. Dawna Markova. I believe that, as the author says, "Random acts of kindness are those little sweet or grand lovely things we do for no reason except that, momentarily, the best of our humanity has sprung, exquisitely into full bloom."

Most of us realize that the world is a difficult place to work in, to live in and to love in. Sometimes I believe that the world sucks and that's why there is a vacuum in outer space.

Yet every time that I get really fed up with human kind, I find a park, a museum, a beautiful picture, hear a beautiful song. Or I have someone spontaneously and wonderfully treat me to a random act of kindness, and my faith in man is immediately restored.

Random acts of kindness are blessings that we humans give to each other; and in that giving, we get more than the person we gave to. Sometimes my perversity makes me send out a random act of kindness.

It is the most fun when I am on a toll road. I'll pull up and give the attendant two dollars instead of one and say, "Hey, I'm paying for the car behind me." That is the best dollar I will spend that day. Imagining the look on the next guy's face is definitely worth 100 pennies.

Handing an old lady I don't know a rose brightens her day and strengthens mine. I can't tell you what random acts of kindness are but there is a checklist in the book I mentioned if you want to learn.

Simply put, they are acts of pure love and gentleness that are performed without any anticipation of reward. In fact, they are best performed anonymously. As an old television commercial used to say, "Try it, you'll like it."

Anderson's Thought

The greatest gifts are the ones we give, not the ones we get.

RULE 25

The most powerful thing in the world is our belief system.

The most powerful thing in the world is our belief system. I think I'll believe in Peter Pan and Fairy Dust and I believe I'll have fun today.

A while back I was in conversation with my wife, Pamela. She is an extremely competent professional and a salesperson beyond compare. She has the best follow-up and problem solving skills with her business clients I've ever seen; but she was feeling anxious, down and was not much fun to be with at that particular time.

She grew up with a work ethic that said, "You are what you do. Your worth as a person is tied to how well you do that job." I understand that concept; it is something that is tied very strongly to the male concept of "I am what I do."

Unfortunately, it was making her and me both miserable. I told her we were going to the movies and she asked, "What are we going to see; another war movie?" I said, "No, we're going to see *Peter Pan*—you need some magic."

Quite frankly, I was concerned about seeing the movie. After Dustin Hoffman and Robin Williams made *Hook* several years ago, I did not think another Peter Pan movie could be made that would adequately tell the story of Peter Pan—I was pleasantly surprised.

Both movies tell the story of believing in magic, what happens when you forget that magic exists and how dangerous that can be. In *Peter Pan*, you learn that fairies are real—as long as you believe in them.

78

You learn that to fly, all you need to do is think happy thoughts. Different people have different things that make them happy; but most importantly, you learn that it is okay to play and have fun! Not only is it okay, it's necessary for finding sanity in an insane world.

In the movie *Hook*, Peter has forgotten who he is and forgets how to play and have fun. In the process of growing up, he became a grown up; and as the story shows, those people can be so stodgy.

Peter was so wrapped up in making a living that he forgot he had a life to live. So often I meet people like that Peter. They did not grow up—they grew old.

I told Pam that the biggest problem she had was that she was married to Peter Pan. I love my life. I love the magical things that come into my life because I believe in magic. I love playing, whether it is with my grandchildren, or my kids, or my wife or my troops (even though I'm retired and don't have troops anymore, I consider them to still be mine).

My granddaughters, Sarah and Rachel, taught me two wonderful lessons when they were just a few years old. Sarah had come over to spend some time with Pam and me and we took her to the Renaissance Festival in Plantersville, Texas. It was amazing; it felt as if we were transported back in time hundreds of years.

For two and a half hours, Pam and I had a great time watching Sarah experience the magic of being young and playing; but eventually Sarah tired out and was grumpy. As we were leaving, a beautiful winged fairy stopped us; and with a purring voice, visited with Sarah who was absolutely enthralled.

The fairy sprinkled fairy dust (or as I prefer to call it—pixie dust) on Sarah and she was good to go for another two hours. I learned that pixie dust (or glitter if you don't believe) was very powerful stuff and I went to the store as soon as we got back to Houston to get me some.

During Sarah's visit, whenever she felt grumpy or was behaving poorly, I'd bring out the pixie dust and everything would change.

Why? Because she believed in the power of pixie dust. That belief gave her permission to behave differently than she felt. As she has grown up, her belief in the "validity" of pixie dust has begun to fall away. That happens when bad things happen to good people. However, she continues to enjoy the magic of make believe because it makes her feel good.

There are enough things in each of our lives to make us feel bad. There is disease, death, taxes, war, abuse, neglect, debt, bankruptcy, divorce—all manner of things that slam into our world and send us spinning off into turmoil.

Those things existed when we were little as well, but we had "make believe" to help us "role play" through the problems. By disassociating ourselves and making catastrophe a learning experience, we developed a plan of attack BEFORE we actually needed one. It was called playing acting and make believe.

I have always said my family has a defective gene—we collect rocks. When Pam and I bought our first home, I put in a rock garden. We convinced the grandkids that this was where we grew rocks.

My second granddaughter, Rachel, came to our house for the first time when she was thirteen months old. Rachel and I would go out to the rock garden four or five times a day—it was Paw Paw time. She would cover her feet and shoes in the rocks and inevitably pick up a rock and move to place it in her mouth. I would say "aaaannngh" and she would stop and put the rock down. We repeated this process four or five times a day for seven days.

On the eighth day, Rachel picked up a rock and stopped before putting it in her mouth and waited on me to say "aaaannngh." On the ninth day, she picked up a rock, covertly threw it away and acted as though she had put it in her mouth and was chewing it.

That showed me that whether you are thirteen months, thirteen years, thirty–three or fifty–three, we are all still children that like to play and see how far we can push the envelope of rules and boundaries.

Most of the lucky ones grow up without growing old—growing up just means that a natural process of maturing has taken place. Growing old means we have lost the ability to play and believe in magic.

Those of us that grow up continue to see possibilities instead of obstacles. We look for new ways to excel instead of settle. We learn that good guys don't always wear white hats and that bad guys don't always wear black.

I have always said, "Live your life like it was a funny book." You have to believe in something, so I have decided to believe in God, believe in magic (which I believe is the fingerprint of God), believe in people, believe in heroes and believe that I will have some fun today—in spite of the world.

Remember that when you believe, an angel gets their wings each time a bell rings, and fairies die if you don't believe in them, and all you have to do to fly is think happy thoughts, and most importantly of all—there's no place like home.

A neat lady named Judi Swalwell reminded me of something one day. I could not leave out her wisdom. She said, "Remember what Dorothy from The Wizard of Oz said, 'If I ever go searching for my heart's desire again, I won't go any further than my own back yard... because if it's not there, I never really lost it to begin with.'"

81

Bob Anderson

Here's to all of us that remember Ruby Slippers.

Anderson's Thought

You can choose to believe in something or nothing. You can choose to find magic in little things or turmoil in big things. It is your choice, make it!

RULE 26

Will power is crap—"Want Power" is what is important in life.

During my years of working with people, I have determined that most folks are well versed in the term will power. Will power is the panacea that everyone believes will solve any insurmountable problem in their lives. They just have to "will" it and it will happen.

After many years of working with drug addicts, I determined that this is a fallacy. Will power is like the unicorn—all of us know what it looks like but none of us has ever seen one. I believe that the most important power any of us possesses is "WANT POWER."

My wife, Pam, says it like this, "Want power means deciding what you want and deciding that any alternative to that, though it may be easier and/or more reasonable, is totally unacceptable."

A while back, I went to the D-Day Museum in New Orleans. There is a wall which portrays the military capabilities of Germany, Japan and, yes, the United States on December 6, 1941. As a military professional and student of the profession of arms, I have never seen such a depressing display.

In my opinion, it is impossible that we should have ever defeated either Japan or Germany, much less both; particularly after December 7, 1941, and the attack on Pearl Harbor. Yet we were victorious. Was it will power? I don't think so.

I am convinced that my father, my uncles and the men and women of the United States military could not have survived on will power. They survived on "Want Power." They wanted to defeat the enemy and come home to their families. They wanted this more than anything else.

I am convinced that the citizens of the United States did not, nearly overnight, create the most impressive industrial program the world has ever seen by will power. They wanted to bring their brothers, sisters, sons, daughters, uncles, husbands, and grandpas home and were willing to do whatever was necessary to accomplish that goal.

That is WANT POWER—not just wanting something to happen but being willing to do whatever is necessary to make it happen. You have to want it more than anything else at that time.

Lastly, I am convinced of the truth of a quote by King Arthur, "Might does not make right; right makes might." Following Pearl Harbor, the Americans felt they were in the right. They wanted the war to end, so they ended it. They did it in spite of the fact that they were initially out gunned, out produced and out-planned.

Quoting Admiral Yamamota, who conceived the attack on Pearl Harbor, "I fear we have only awakened a sleeping giant and filled him with a terrible resolve." He was right!

To win that war, the sailors, soldiers and airman, Marines and Coast Guard had to fight to win—and they did. The home folks had to sacrifice to give our service members the ammunition, weapons and supplies to win—and they did.

They did not want to fight the Germans or the Japanese over there; but more than that, they did not want to fight them over here, and they were willing to do what it took to keep that from happening. They just wanted peace, so they fought for it—that is WANT POWER.

We live in a country where if you want something and you are strong enough to pursue it, you are willing to do what is necessary to have it, you are willing to overcome obstacles, you are

willing to be responsible and you are willing to be held accountable—you will attain it. If you don't, it is probably because you
decided your goal was completely unreasonable and you quit.

I quote Sir Winston Churchill who led Great Britain through
the Second World War. During the days when the buzz bombs
were falling on London, after the British Army was evacuated
from Dunkirk and when the very life of England was threatened
by the approaching forces of Germany, he spoke these words:
"Never, in all things, large or small—never, never quit."

Anderson's Thought

*What I want is within my power, if it only requires my effort;
and if I want it bad enough.*

RULE 27

Living is like sharpening a knife.

"Do you know how to sharpen a knife?" You rub it against something that is harder than the knife. You must have the right angle. You must balance the number of strokes on each side of the blade or the edge will not be even.

The same applies to us as people. Find something or someone that is "harder" than you are and try your best to incorporate those good qualities into yourself.

Get the right "angle." That angle will always be how you can serve someone else, not yourself. Find the "balance" by doing right things, the right way, every day.

Some people, like George King, will come into your life and "sharpen" you by showing you how to live. Some people will come into your life and "sharpen" you by showing you how NOT to live. Both can teach you; one is just more fun than the other.

As I've previously stated, adults learn faster by trying to avoid pain and embarrassment than by any other method. As also previously stated, "We learn nothing from our successes; we are not supposed to. We are supposed to celebrate them."

We only learn from those things at which we fail, those things that cause pain and embarrassment. Children learn slowly by their successes. Older folks learn faster by learning how to avoid punishment, embarrassment and failure. Fortunately, or unfortunately, it is the way of things.

As I said before, I have often pondered the question, "What would you change in your life?" Like most folks, for years I contemplated what would I change if I could go back in time.

87

What mistakes would I not make? What could I do to avoid hurting the people I have hurt? What disasters would I be able to avoid?

Then I came to realize that all of the things I would like to change or avoid or should have prevented, were part of what has made me who I am today.

Everything that has come into my life—every friend, every enemy, every opportunity, every failure, every accomplishment, every embarrassment, every goal achieved and every goal denied, have all worked together to make me exactly who I am at this moment.

This is particularly true of those things that I would consider negative in my life. Again, I do not believe we learn from successes, we celebrate them.

Some folks do not learn from their failures either but I have tried. I think for the most part, I have succeeded.

I have learned that everyone has the potential for making mistakes. I have learned that society is not the best determinate of my behavior—I am. I have learned that I could lie, cheat, steal, lust, betray friends and seek comfort from my enemies.

I have learned that integrity is only integrity as long as it is protected and defended. I have learned that fear can be a friend; it keeps you from being stupid. I have learned that courage is not the absence of fear; rather it is the controlling of that fear.

In the "old days," bad things happened to good people. People were expected and required to "get past" those bad things. Previous generations recognized that individual events were a poor standard by which to evaluate life. Invariably, people grew stronger for having combated the negative forces they encountered.

During the sixties, we began to realize that events and tragedies had a tremendous impact on human beings. Those impacts could last for days, months, years; or in some cases, remain for a life time.

We discovered that the "combat fatigue" experienced by soldiers during World War II and previous conflicts, was better named "Post Traumatic Shock Syndrome."

My Dad, like many soldiers from World War II, saw horrific things. He felt fear. He saw friends killed in front of his own eyes. He carried those images with him until the day he died but he, like many other men and women who are placed in traumatic conditions, did his very best to "get past" those isolated and terrible events. He decided that he would not let those terrible events define his life.

Rather, he would use those terrible events to help refine his life. There was no way to stop the visions, but he learned to deal with them as dreams, horrible memories; but just that— memories.

The memory is a magical thing. A song, a scent or a sight can instantly transport a human mind through days, years or decades to a previous event. And while the human mind explores the reliving of that event, the event is almost real again. The operative phrase is "almost."

It is a condition of living that we humans will suffer. It is a condition of living that we humans will fail. It is a condition of living that terrible things will happen that can affect us for a long time.

It is also a condition of living that we humans will prevail. It is a condition of living that we humans will succeed. It is a condition of living that wonderful things will happen that can affect us for a long time.

Our job as humans is to determine where we will focus our attention and our intention. Santayana said, "He who fails to remember the past is destined to repeat it." He was correct but I would add, "He who fails to remember the past and learn from it, will repeat the past."

The definition of crazy is doing the same thing again and again and again and again the same way, and expecting it to turn out differently. Avoiding this trap requires experience and evaluation and a change in actions and thoughts that will allow for success.

This is where the analogy of knife sharpening comes in. The knife becomes sharper by rubbing it against something that is harder than it is, the correct way and the correct number of times on each side.

I have accomplished many things in my life that I am proud of but there are also things in my life that I am deeply ashamed of. It is that shame that keeps me from doing things I was able to justify in the past.

It is not so much that I enjoy living in the wonderful light I have found. More so, it is that I never want to go back into the darkness of where I was.

If you read this and the message resonates with you and you are in that darkness, know that you have chosen that pit you are in and you can choose to climb out of it.

If you are reading this and you are someone I have wronged in the past, please accept my sincerest and most heartfelt apology. Please know there is not a day that goes by I don't think of the wrongs I did.

That constant memory has molded my behavior and my life and by not doing that to anyone else, I am better. God bless all of you that have come into my life and been a sharpening stone for me. Thank you.

Anderson's Thought

I am who I am not because of what happened to me, but because of how I chose to be and act after it happened.
"Don't cry because it is over; smile because it happened."

—Dr.Seuss

ABOUT THE AUTHOR

Bob is a speaker and avid writer. As a speaker, his power message advocates doing hard things, especially when it's unpopular or uncomfortable to do so; simple and back to basics. He believes in unwavering commitment and courage. He believes success is earned, not given; it's a privilege, not a right.

Bob retired as a Chief Master Sergeant from the United States Air Force Reserve (USAFR) with over 32 years of service.

He is co-author of **The Survivalist** series with Jerry and Sharon Ahern (starting with book #30). Additionally he's the author of the **TAC Leader** series, **Sarge**, **What Now?**, **Grandfather Speaks** and **Anderson's Rules**.

Bob is a qualified rappel master, holds a 2nd degree black belt in karate, and is an expert in weaponry and military tactics. He and his wife, Pamela, reside in Missouri.

A Note from the Author

Anderson's Rules is about success and the elements of living that make life fun and fulfilling. It was both fun and challenging to write. One of the main reasons I wrote this book was to honor folks that have come into my life and had an impact on me.

I have discovered that most things in living can be broken down into terms that are relative to the martial arts and the Eastern philosophy known as Zen. The philosophy can best be expressed by the words, "What is—is. Therefore, what is not—is not."

I would appreciate your comments on the story. I hope that ***Anderson's Rules*** offers food for your soul. I hope it offers you challenge. Each of us goes through life as individuals that some-times can share a moment, an experience or a lifetime with another person. I hope our moments together was of value for you.

Following is a short selection of topics that I present on a reg-ular basis as a professional speaker. These presentations are designed to help create better leaders and followers; both person-ally and professionally.

- Excellence Ain't Easy! (Personal Development)
- Can You Shoot Your Own Dog? (Leadership)
- You Can't See-saw By Yourself! (Teamwork)
- Say What? (Effective Communications)
- Everything and More! (Personal Development)

If you would like me to do a presentation regarding the ideas set forth in this book, please contact me through my website at www.BobAndersonBooks.com. I would love the opportunity to meet you.

Bob

www.ingramcontent.com/pod-product-compliance
Lightning Source LLC
LaVergne TN
LVHW091159080426
835509LV00006B/749